T0279885

WHAT CAN WE HOPE FOR?

WHAT CAN WE HOPE FOR?

ESSAYS ON POLITICS

RICHARD RORTY

Edited by W. P. Malecki and Chris Voparil

PRINCETON UNIVERSITY PRESS

PRINCETON & OXFORD

Published by Princeton University Press
41 William Street, Princeton, New Jersey 08540
99 Banbury Road, Oxford OX2 6JX

press.princeton.edu

Library of Congress Cataloging-in-Publication Data

Names: Rorty, Richard, author. | Małecki, Wojciech (Professor of literary theory), editor. | Voparil, Christopher J., 1969– editor.
Title: What can we hope for? : essays on politics / Richard Rorty ; edited by W.P. Malecki and Chris Voparil.
Description: Princeton, New Jersey : Princeton University Press, 2022. | Includes bibliographical references and index.
Identifiers: LCCN 2021034288 (print) | LCCN 2021034289 (ebook) | ISBN 9780691217529 (acid-free paper) | ISBN 9780691217536 (ebook)
Subjects: LCSH: Political culture—United States. | Democracy. | Globalization—Political aspects.
Classification: LCC JK1726 .R727 2022 (print) | LCC JK1726 (ebook) | DDC 320.973—dc23
LC record available at https://lccn.loc.gov/2021034288
LC ebook record available at https://lccn.loc.gov/2021034289

British Library Cataloging-in-Publication Data is available

Editorial: Rob Tempio, Matt Rohal, and Chloe Coy
Production Editorial: Natalie Baan
Text Design: Karl Spurzem
Jacket Design: Lauren Michelle Smith
Production: Erin Suydam
Publicity: Carmen Jimenez and James Schneider
Copyeditor: Hank Southgate

This book has been composed in Arno

10 9 8 7 6 5 4 3 2 1

For

Antoni, Julia, and Pola
Aidan and Devin

What matters for pragmatists is devising ways of diminishing human suffering and increasing human equality, increasing the ability of all children to start life with an equal chance of happiness.

—RICHARD RORTY

CONTENTS

ACKNOWLEDGMENTS

We are grateful for Mary Varney Rorty's unwavering support for this project. The final version in your hands benefited significantly from the insightful eye of Rob Tempio at Princeton University Press, whose enthusiasm and encouragement—and good humor—were crucial throughout the process, and from helpful comments from two anonymous reviewers. Our thanks go to Matt Rohal and the fine editorial staff who saw the manuscript to fruition, and to the staff of the UC Irvine Special Collections and Archives, Critical Theory Archive, where the Richard Rorty Papers are located, in particular to Steven McLeod and Audra Eagle Yun. We also want to acknowledge the countless colleagues who have shared their wisdom about Rorty's political thought with us over the years. There are too many to list, but we must thank Dick Bernstein, Eduardo Mendieta, and the members of the Richard Rorty Society. Our hope is that this volume of Rorty's crucial and still timely writings on politics shall stimulate commitment to continuing his unfinished pragmatist project of diminishing human suffering and increasing human equality for generations to come.

NOTE ON SOURCES

Most of the essays included in this volume were previously published, as listed below. Four essays are based on electronic documents from the "born-digital" archive of the Richard Rorty Papers, MS-C017, Special Collections and Archives, The UC Irvine Libraries, Irvine, California, http://ucispace.lib.uci.edu /handle/10575/7. In the following, we provide what we have been able to gather about dates and occasions of the unpublished papers.

Our minimal editorial interventions in preparing the unpublished manuscripts fell into two categories. First, we removed the obvious traces of the papers' original contexts of presentation. For instance, the original text for the lecture "American Universities and the Hope for Social Justice" included "in the time that remains," which we altered to "in the space that remains." These editorial interventions were limited to *obvious* traces of oral presentation that could be changed without affecting the content and tone of the text. We did not intervene in the style or syntax. The second type of intervention relates to Rorty's famous habit of name-dropping, where he would simply say that a given thinker claims p or q without giving any reference to the relevant work by that author or even his or her first name. Normally, an editor's job would be to locate the relevant source and add the first name of a given author when he or she is cited the first time. However, since Rorty's practice of name-dropping was a characteristic element of his style, we usually chose not to do so. The exceptions were cases where, for example, in "Back to Class Politics," Rorty alludes to "as John Sweeney reminds us in his book" with no citation, presumably because he assumed an audience's awareness at the time. In cases like this, we decided to add references to the works Rorty most likely had in mind, distinguishing our footnotes from Rorty's with "—Eds."

1. "Who Are We? Moral Universalism and Economic Triage" appeared in *Diogenes* 173 (1996): 5–15. Reprinted with permission of Sage Publishing.

2. "Democracy and Philosophy" was published in *Kritika & Kontext* 33 (2007): 8–25. Reprinted with permission from the Estate of Richard Rorty.

3. "Dewey and Posner on Pragmatism and Moral Progress" was published in the *University of Chicago Law Review* 74, no. 3 (2007): 915–27. We gratefully acknowledge permission to reprint.

4. "Rethinking Democracy" (1996). Manuscript reproduced with permission from the Estate of Richard Rorty.

5. "First Projects, Then Principles" appeared in *The Nation*, May 19, 1997, 9. We gratefully acknowledge permission to reprint.

6. "Does Being an American Give One a Moral Identity?" (1998). Manuscript reproduced with permission from the Estate of Richard Rorty.

7. "Demonizing the Academy" was published in *Harper's Magazine*, January 1995, 13–17. Reprinted with permission from the Estate of Richard Rorty. A slightly modified version appears in the *Journal of Blacks in Higher*

Education, no. 7 (Spring 1995): 74–75, under the title
"The Demonization of Multiculturalism."

8. "American Universities and the Hope for Social Justice"
   (2001). Manuscript reproduced with permission from
   the Estate of Richard Rorty.

9. "The Intellectuals and the Poor" (1996). Manuscript
   reproduced with permission from the Estate of Richard
   Rorty. This text is based on a lecture given at Pomona
   College on February 19, 1996. There are two additional
   versions in the archive, edited by Rorty himself in 1997
   and in 2001. This version is based on the 2001 text, with
   unfinished portions and a separate opening section
   omitted.

10. "Can American Egalitarianism Survive a Globalized
    Economy?" appeared in the *Ruffin Series of the Society
    for Business Ethics* 1 (1998): 1–6, https://doi.org/10.5840
    /ruffinx199819. We gratefully acknowledge permission
    to reprint.

11. "Back to Class Politics" was published in *Dissent* 44, no. 1
    (Winter 1997): 31–34 (and later included in *Philosophy
    and Social Hope* [New York: Penguin Books, 1999],
    255–61). It was adopted from a speech Rorty gave at
    the Columbia University Teach-In with the Labor
    Movement on October 3, 1996. Reprinted with permission
    of the University of Pennsylvania Press.

12. "Making the Rich Richer" is an op-ed piece published
    in the *New York Times* on March 6, 2000. We gratefully
    acknowledge permission to reprint.

13 "Looking Backwards from the Year 2096" first appeared
    as "Fraternity Reigns" in the *New York Times* magazine on
    September 29, 1996, 155, and was reprinted as "Looking
    Backwards from the Year 2096" in *Philosophy and Social*

Hope (New York: Penguin Books, 1999), 243–51. Reprinted with permission from the Estate of Richard Rorty.

14. "The Unpredictable American Empire" was published in *Pragmatism, Nation, and Race: Community in the Age of Empire,* ed. Chad Kautzer and Eduardo Mendieta (Bloomington: Indiana University Press, 2009), 209–21. Reprinted with permission of Indiana University Press.

15. "Post-Democracy: Anti-Terrorism and the National Security State" appeared in the *London Review of Books,* April 1, 2004, 10–11. Reprinted with permission from the Estate of Richard Rorty.

16. "Humiliation or Solidarity? The Hope for a Common European Foreign Policy" was published in *Dissent* 50, no. 4 (Fall 2003): 23–36. Reprinted with permission of the University of Pennsylvania Press.

17. "Half a Million Blue Helmets?" appeared in *Common Knowledge* 4, no. 3 (1995): 10–13. Copyright 1995 Duke University Press, www.dukeupress.edu. All rights reserved. Republished by permission of the copyright holder.

18. "A Queasy Agnosticism," a review of Ian McEwan's *Saturday,* came out in *Dissent* 50, no. 4 (Fall 2005): 91–94. Reprinted with permission of the University of Pennsylvania Press.

Afterword. "Intellectuals and the Millennium" was published in *New Leader,* February 24, 1997, 10–11. Reprinted with permission from the Estate of Richard Rorty.

WHAT CAN WE HOPE FOR?

INTRODUCTION

THE PHILOSOPHER AND HIS COUNTRY

W. P. Malecki and Chris Voparil

Richard Rorty (1931–2007) is best known to the wider public as the philosopher who predicted Trump. During the 2016 presidential election, eerily prescient warnings from his 1998 book, *Achieving Our Country*, that existing forces of American politics might set the country on a road to fascism, went viral on social media. With neither the left nor the right showing concern for the growing economic disparities in America, he contended in 1998, a large swath of voters already experiencing the negative impact of globalization would become acutely disillusioned with the political establishment. Suffering from economic inequality and insecurity, these mostly white, working-class citizens would feel that they had nowhere to turn for advocacy on their behalf, since conservatives had neglected their interests and liberals were rejecting their values.

"At that point, something will crack," he prophesied, and "the nonsuburban electorate would decide that the system had failed." They would start looking around for a populist "strongman" who would pay homage to their fears. He would be elected to the Oval Office and ultimately roll back the progressive achievements of the previous decades. "Jocular contempt for women," Rorty predicted, would come back into vogue, along with racial and ethnic epithets thought to have been defeated. "Media-created pseudo-events, including the occasional brief and bloody war," would be manufactured to distract citizens from exploitation by the "super-rich" and "the resentment which badly educated Americans feel about having their manners dictated to them by college graduates" would be stoked. "This strongman leader, he concluded, "will be a disaster for the country and the world."[1]

The same premises that led Rorty to predict Trump generated other predictions and warnings: predictions about a new civil war in America, a new feudalism in the West, and a new, brutal world order resulting from global overpopulation. These potential outcomes are universally grim and look even more probable now than when Rorty first envisioned them. He may well turn out to be the philosopher who predicted not only the 2016 election but the political upheavals still ahead of us.

This book gathers these and other Rortyan prophecies about the dark and disturbing currents still coursing through the bodies politic in America and around the globe. It also contains essays that show that, if he were alive today, Rorty would be uneasy about the label "the philosopher who predicted Trump." Not because it diminishes the contributions to perennial philosophical subjects that made him one of the most cited American thinkers of the twentieth century. Quite the contrary, he would be uneasy about the label because, judged from the theoretical perspective he advocated, it makes his philosophical contributions look too important. It suggests that he predicted Trump thanks to some superior philosophical acumen and thereby strengthens the traditional image of philosophers as people whose special expertise allows them to see the world more clearly than everyone else. Rorty believed that image to be mistaken and argued that taking it seriously was one of the reasons why the American academic left, which he believed to be "overphilosophized," was failing miserably. These diagnoses and critiques, still of enormous relevance to understanding how the contemporary left, in the United States and elsewhere, has boxed itself into a corner, are included here as well.

What Can We Hope For? also conveys Rorty's pragmatic philosophy of democratic change. It contains his recommendations for concrete reforms to ameliorate injustice and inequality and his positive vision for what safeguarding our democracy and our highest aspirations requires. He understood that the integrity of democracy depends on stable and secure institutions like a free press, a free judiciary, and free elections. He also grasped that democracy requires a moral community that must be actively cultivated, grounded in our sense of who we and our fellow citizens are and should become. These essays outline Rorty's strategies—more timely now than ever—for fostering social hope and building an inclusive global community of trust.

Rorty's Life and Ideas

Richard McKay Rorty was born on October 4, 1931. He was an intellectually precocious child who demonstrated an early facility with language. At the age of six, he composed a historical play, and at seven wrote the Harvard College Observatory to inquire about becoming an astronomer.[2] A self-described "nerdy recluse and fighter for social justice," he was a shy and awkward kid who took refuge in books and solo excursions into the northwest New Jersey woods in search of elusive wild orchids.[3] His moral compass received its bearing from his parents' committed leftist activism. At twelve, he lent a hand at the Workers

Defense League in New York City, where his parents worked, by carrying press releases via subway to A. Phillip Randolph's office at the Brotherhood of Pullman Car Porters, carefully reading them along the way. As Rorty later put it, "I grew up knowing that all decent people were, if not Trotskyites, at least socialists."[4] His father, James Rorty, the son of an Irish immigrant, was an author, poet, and muckraking journalist who was awarded a Distinguished Service Cross for his service in World War I as an unarmed stretcher-bearer. His mother, Winifred Raushenbush, the daughter of social gospel theologian Walter Rauschenbusch, studied sociology at the University of Chicago with George Herbert Mead and Robert Park and was a published writer herself.

At fifteen, Rorty enrolled in the University of Chicago's "Hutchins College," where he rubbed shoulders with students who would become important figures in American intellectual life, including Allan Bloom. His goal, at that point in life, was to find a way, in Yeats's phrase, "to hold reality and justice in a single vision," that is, to encounter a convincing intellectual rationale that would justify his high-minded intellectual interests as integral to the quest for social justice, which he understood as "the liberation of the weak from the strong."[5] Though he soon gave up the project of reconciliation—he was unable to convince himself to follow Plato in holding that knowledge was virtue—he remained at Chicago to complete a master's degree in philosophy and write a thesis on Alfred North Whitehead. Rorty continued his studies at Yale University, where he received his PhD in philosophy in 1956. After a brief stint in the US army, Rorty taught for twenty years at Princeton University before moving in 1982 to the University of Virginia and then to Stanford in 1998, where he remained until retirement in 2005. He succumbed to pancreatic cancer on June 8, 2007.

Rorty's philosophy is most closely associated with the tradition of American pragmatism. This constellation of ideas emphasizing the unity of thought and action and the primacy of practice emerges in the last quarter of the nineteenth century in writings of Charles Sanders Peirce that were popularized by William James and developed with different variations by John Dewey, Josiah Royce, Jane Addams, Alain Locke, and others during the first half of the twentieth century. In recent years, pragmatism has been advanced by Cornel West and Robert Brandom, both former students of Rorty's, and also enjoys a place in many disciplines outside philosophy. Rorty wasn't always linked to pragmatism. For the first two decades of his career, his professional standing was owed to a series of essays in the late 1960s and early 1970s on technical topics within mainstream analytic philosophy, the dominant mode of the discipline, then as now, which largely rejected pragmatism for being too quaint and muddled to meet the demands of logically rigorous philosophical inquiry.

One of Rorty's insights in his groundbreaking book, *Philosophy and the Mirror of Nature* (1979), was to discern a gradual pragmaticization of analytic philosophy. Mid-twentieth-century thinkers like W. V. O Quine and Wilfrid Sellars had initiated critiques that Rorty developed into a major challenge to the fundamental assumptions of the Cartesian-Kantian tradition's conceptions of mind, philosophy, and knowledge. Rejecting the idea that these views are intrinsic to the nature of reality or our essential human nature, Rorty contended that they are no more than contingent, historically rooted metaphors that we can alter when they outlive their usefulness. Over the years that followed, he relentlessly critiqued commitments that philosophers held dear: the idea that true beliefs mirror reality in itself, the notion of Philosophy, with a capital "p," as a privileged discipline with special access to The Way Things Are, and the idea that our culture and democracy are in need of philosophical foundations or "backup" to sustain them. Rorty advanced a program of "therapeutic" rather than "constructive" philosophy that aimed to be "edifying" rather than "systematic" by freeing us from reliance on outdated metaphors and on nonhuman sources of authority to validate our beliefs. The goal was to foster human moral progress to accompany the historical transition from religion to philosophy to literature as the center of Western culture.[6]

Alongside this critical project, Rorty developed an alternative positive vision based on a radical shift: "putting politics first and tailoring a philosophy to suit."[7] If leading philosophical vocabularies obstruct rather than advance our democratic aims, we should drop them for more useful ones. Hope replaces transcendental knowledge, a possible future takes the place of appeals to an eternal reality, stories supplant philosophical arguments, and abstract notions of humanity and rights are abandoned for felt, emotional identifications with particular communities. In *Contingency, Irony, and Solidarity* (1989), he outlined the implications of his pragmatism for how we understand language, selfhood, and community, and he experimented with a form of cultural criticism that embodied "a general turn against theory and toward narrative," inviting "genres such as ethnography, the journalist's report, the comic book, the docudrama, and, especially, the novel" into the conversation.[8] "If we take care of freedom," he famously asserted, "truth can take care of itself."[9] The only grounding liberal democracy needs is a shared commitment to reduce cruelty and suffering.

These pioneering efforts were greeted with dismissive criticism and charges of relativism, irrationalism, even irresponsibility, for allegedly severing us from the independent standards and external checks needed to keep our beliefs from falling into error. Only with time did a fuller understanding emerge that Rorty's philosophico-political project constitutes nothing less than a large-scale program for self-criticism and reform of Western societies by modifying their "self-image" to make them more responsive to suffering and injustice, both at home and abroad. Rorty's politics remained largely static over the course of his lifetime and philosophical trajectory. Biographer Neil Gross concluded that Rorty's "intellectual self-concept of leftist American patriot," acquired in large part from his parents, was reinspired in the wake of their deaths in the 1970s and the rise of the New Left.[10] While Rorty consistently insisted that there is no necessary link from his or anyone's philosophical critiques of truth, rationality, and objectivity to liberal democracy, he did believe that "there is a plausible inference from democratic convictions" to such philosophical views.[11] The affinity stems from a moral commitment to "antiauthoritarianism," his name for the pragmatist objection to any form of fundamentalism, whether philosophical or religious, that attempts "to circumvent the process of achieving democratic consensus" by appealing to "the authority of something 'not ourselves.'"[12] In Rorty's antiauthoritarian vision, "Both monotheism and the kind of metaphysics or science that purports to tell you what the world *really* is like are replaced with democratic politics."[13]

These commitments illuminate two registers of politics that exist in Rorty's writings. The first, which he once dubbed "real politics," involves organized efforts to reduce economic inequality, provide basic needs, and improve people's lives in banal ways through things like labor unions, coalitions, policy reforms, and changing laws. The second register is alluded to in the last volume of essays completed in his lifetime, *Philosophy as Cultural Politics* (2007), which makes the case that intervening in "cultural politics" should be philosophers' "principal assignment."[14] This apparent embrace of "cultural politics" was surprising to readers of Achieving Our Country familiar with Rorty's scathing indictment of the "academic, cultural Left" for its dismissal of "real" politics and "mock[ing] the very idea that democratic institutions might once again be made to serve social justice."[15] However, his later return to "cultural politics" invokes instead the register of politics oriented to the broad, generational cultural change highlighted in Rorty's work of the 1980s of "liberating the culture from obsolete vocabularies" and "reweaving of the community's fabric of belief" so that we get to "the point where we treat everything—our language, our conscience, our community—as a product of time and chance."[16] For philosophers to intervene in cultural politics, in this sense, is to join poets and novelists and other social critics in offering new vocabularies and imagining new ways of looking at the world: "social hopes, programs of action, and prophecies of a better future."[17]

If Rorty's major philosophical contributions revived the ideas of classical pragmatism, his major political contributions rejuvenated the priorities of the "reformist Left," his label for US figures from the Progressive Era to the Vietnam War who worked for democratic change within the system, like Eugene Debs, Irving Howe, and A. Phillip Randolph Jr., among many others. This political orientation was not only quite rare at the time when Rorty wrote, but put him at odds with both the left and the right of his day.

For instance, if the right thought capitalism a perfectly just economic arrangement needing only to be freed from externally imposed limitations and the left thought it the worst of all possible systems that must be abolished right now, Rorty believed that while capitalism definitely generates all sorts of injustices, no viable economic alternatives currently exist. As a result, the only option is to make capitalism more humane by tinkering with its details—for example, by introducing on a global scale the economic mechanisms that make countries like Norway or Sweden economically successful welfare states. To take another example, if the right believed that one should love America unconditionally because of its greatness and the left believed that it is impossible to love America at all because of its injustices, Rorty opted for a difficult love instead. That is, he argued that one should both remember the country's political sins and appreciate its great achievements. Without the former one will not know what needs to be changed, and without the latter one will lack the necessary motivation for the task. As to what needs to be changed, while the left believed that political attention should be turned to the rights of the oppressed and the right thought those could be left out of politics altogether, Rorty believed that such rights mattered a great deal, but not in the way the left thought they did. While the left focused on the politics of recognition, where each and every cultural difference should be celebrated, Rorty emphasized the politics of anti-discrimination, or making sure that nobody has to suffer just because they are different.

Stated this way, Rorty's political orientation may look quite clear, but it has been very often dramatically misunderstood. His attacking both sides in many a contemporary political debate was easily mistaken as supporting one side or the other. For instance, while he attacked the right for its lack of concern for social justice, he often was seen as a representative of the radical cultural left he in fact opposed. While he attacked the left for its revolutionist yearnings and lack of patriotism, his stance often was taken to be rightist and dubbed "altogether appropriate for the age of Reagan."[18] Rorty was troubled by both kinds of misinterpretation, but it was the latter that really hurt him. His gripe with the left, after all, was not about principles and ideals, but merely about how best to realize them in practice. He shared its unconditional commitment to social justice just as he shared its vision of a classless society where nobody has to suffer economic hardship and discrimination is gone forever. He just thought the left's ideas about how to get there were mostly wrong—ineffective at best and dangerous at worst. His famed Trump prediction was precisely an attempt to point out one such danger. Indeed, all his political essays were written in this pragmatic mode. Their underlying intention, seen clearly throughout this volume, was to point out concrete problems and possibilities, and to propose concrete solutions.

Overview of Contents

The essays of part I explain why Rorty adopted this pragmatic approach even though one might expect something quite different from a philosopher. Philosophers, after all, traditionally have busied themselves with providing theoretical foundations for politics rather than with practical details of how politics should be done. Many even have believed that without first answering the primordial philosophical question "What are we?" about the true nature of human beings, it is simply impossible to answer the primordial political question "*Who* are we?" about what kind of community humanity should ideally become. In chapter 1, Rorty argues that this approach has things exactly backward. Instead of the philosophical question "What are we?" coming first and the political question "Who are we?" second, he holds that all responses to "What are we?" are concealed answers to the question "Who are we?" The question of what sort of community we should ideally be is therefore not

THE PHILOSOPHER AND HIS COUNTRY 11

only the primordial political question but the primordial philosophical one as well. Rorty then proceeds to argue that forming a political community necessarily entails providing an ideal that spurs its members to accept certain moral obligations toward one another, such as the obligation to help those in need. But to actually belong to a political community, it is not enough simply to accept one's moral obligations toward certain people. One must also be convinced that one can fulfill them. The question whether we can help others, he concludes, is therefore not merely a question of what we can do, but of who we really are. To answer it, philosophy should turn away from its traditional subject, the eternal, and look toward the future, asking itself another pragmatic question: "What may we hope?"

If the first chapter stresses that politics is of fundamental importance to philosophy, the ones that follow suggest that, contrary to what many philosophers believe, philosophy is of little importance to politics. Such belief, he explains in "Democracy and Philosophy," is a relic of the eighteenth century, when the importance of philosophy for politics was indeed enormous. Those who wanted to substitute secular democracy for the ancien régime were unable to appeal to factual evidence, since no egalitarian democracies existed. Instead, they relied on abstract philosophical arguments that used materialist premises to attack the theological foundations of the old regime. Today, however, there is no real need to resort to such measures in debating politics. There is enough factual data available on the merits and demerits of the major positions involved for that to seem necessary or even helpful.

"Dewey and Posner on Pragmatism and Moral Progress" offers a cogent statement of how Rorty understands philosophy's relation to politics via his hero John Dewey's conception of philosophy as "a social hope reduced to a working program of action, a prophecy of the future."[19] On this view, what sustains democracy is not a grounding in truth or metaphysics or other form of specialized knowledge from which we can deduce philosophical justifications that validate our beliefs as correct. Here Rorty agrees with legal philosopher Richard Posner, who has held that such epistemological defenses miss the point that "consensus makes 'truth' rather than truth forcing consensus."[20] In other words, the mere existence of truth or facts, as recent political discourse attests, does not automatically generate consensus. On the contrary, agreement with our fellow citizens is an ongoing task that must be actively pursued. Rational arguments and appeals to first principles get no traction when participants lack a background of shared premises. In these moments, we must look to "nonrational" methods, Rorty says, like those practiced by Martin Luther King Jr., Betty Friedan, and the leaders of the gay rights movement. They brought about change by expanding our moral imaginations and asking us to care about those who were suffering. In short, "They incited social hope by proposing programs of action, and by prophesying a better future."[21]

"Rethinking Democracy" responds to challenges to democratic politics that allegedly flow from postmodern philosophy on the one hand and current global crises on the other. The former challenges lie in postmodernism's critique of the universality of norms, including any norms underlying democracy, and the latter challenges reside in the fact that the measures thought to be necessary to address current global crises are unlikely to gain assent through democratic procedures. Taken together, these considerations seemingly force us to rethink democracy. Rorty thinks there is no need to do any such thing. Instead, we should abandon the outdated assumption that democracy needs universal moral norms as its foundation.

Existing evidence for the practical superiority of democracy to any other imaginable system is foundation enough, as well as reason enough, to keep democracy in place despite current crises. Instead of rethinking democracy, then, we need to rethink the solutions to our current problems so that they could be realized through democratic measures. The final essay of part I, "First Projects, Then Principles," argues that this can be done without reconciling conflicting beliefs if we can find projects capable of garnering wide participation.

The remaining chapters of the book develop this credo in response to leading political matters of Rorty's day. His analyses and calls for change continue to resonate. Part II is devoted to the US context, beginning with "Does Being an American Give One a Moral Identity?" a previously unpublished essay that offers Rorty's most in-depth account of how moral identity and group membership structure our positions on political questions. He counsels his fellow Americans "to incorporate our . . . citizenship into our moral identities" as the prerequisite for successful collective self-reform.[22]

The three essays that follow offer the most sustained expression of Rorty's views on the historical achievements of universities, and the contemporary problems and excesses that must be overcome for them to realize their promise for vouchsafing democracy's future. "Demonizing the Academy" predicts that the years ahead are likely to see "more and more attempts to discredit the colleges and universities, for the right is well aware that the American academy is now (after the breakdown of the labor movement) the last remaining defender of the poor against the rich and of the weak against the strong." Rorty pierces the right's false narrative of leftist academics run amok, recognizing that while they might manage "to get control of a primary school system here and a university English department

there, the well-organized, well-financed, and very energetic religious right is a hundred times more threatening to free speech
and diversity of opinion than all the [academic leftists] put together." For all the right's doomsaying about universities teem-
ing with leftists, the latter's members are far fewer than the right
imagines. Always managing to rile both left and right, he also
chafes against "facile exercises in 'sensitivity'" that fail to promote "genuine discussion about the divisions in American
society [that] would concentrate on disparities of power rather
than differences in culture."[23] For Rorty, racism, rather than a
failure to recognize cultural diversity, is the deeper injustice in
need of redress.

In "American Universities and the Hope for Social Justice"
and "The Intellectuals and the Poor," both of which appear here
in print for the first time, Rorty addresses the nature and limits
of what universities and intellectuals can contribute to the
cause of social justice, taking up still timely topics like attitudes
toward populism and the growing anti-intellectual backlash
generated by the sneering attitude of self-appointed political
correctness police. Learning from William James's insights into
the "ethos" of certain academic departments' growing remove
from the broader US culture, Rorty grasps that the university's
claim to being the moral conscience of the nation only holds
when it resists disdain. He calls for a sober recognition of the
United States' historical injustices, without allowing shame
over the past to morph into either an anti-Americanism that
encourages its victims "to turn their backs on the country than
to claim a share in its history and future," or receptivity to the
right's narrative of white grievance that aims only to divide
Americans from each other.[24]

Rorty nevertheless refuses to voice mere jeremiads. He con-
nects his diagnoses to concrete reform efforts that offer potential

common ground, like the "justice for janitors" movement on college campuses in "American Universities and the Hope for Social Justice" and policy proposals for the Social Security Administration in "Making the Rich Richer." "Can American Egalitarianism Survive a Globalized Economy?" and "Back to Class Politics" speak directly to the plight of the US working class and the widening gap between rich and poor that only has worsened since Rorty wrote. The latter essay brings the issue of racial injustice into the conversation about globalization in ways that many accounts, including others of Rorty's own, fail to do. The section closes with Rorty's dystopian narrative "Looking Backwards from the Year 2096," which dramatizes the perils of failing to think of each other as fellow citizens, a danger more severe now than ever that, according to the essay, may lead America on a downward spiral from social unrest through a new civil war all the way to "the dark years" of military dictatorship.

Rorty's orthodoxy-bashing and divide-bridging continue in part III's turn to global issues. "The Unpredictable American Empire" charts a course between those who would condemn America irredeemably for its imperialism and those who uncritically exalt its exceptionalism. "Post-Democracy" worries about authoritarian regimes exploiting the threat of terrorism to curtail democratic freedoms and portends a rise of neofeudalism in Western democracies, before offering practical remedies. Both essays sound the refrain of "Rethinking Democracy" that what is needed is a renewal of our democratic faith and not a questioning of democracy. In "Humiliation or Solidarity?" Rorty joins European intellectuals Jürgen Habermas and Jacques Derrida in addressing the role and importance of a unified Europe, a topic given new urgency by Brexit. His call for an international police force in "Half a Million Blue Helmets?" capable of being deployed to quell local armed gangs whose violence can escalate into ethnic cleansing responds to an on-the-ground need conveyed to him on a visit to Serbia, a stance unlikely to earn him allies on the left. "A Queasy Agnosticism" is a timely reflection, spurred by Ian McEwan's novel *Saturday*, on the declining hegemony of the West and the possibility that, as hope is increasingly replaced by fear, the West may betray its own ideals. The resulting inability "to sketch a credible agenda for large-scale change" constitutes a profound problem insofar as our growing queasiness about the level of injustice we currently tolerate makes it "hard to find inspiration in a vision of a just, free, global community."[25]

The volume concludes with "Intellectuals and the Millennium," Rorty's forward-looking take on the prospects for moral and political progress globally that expresses his view that further progress should lie not in philosophy or religion, but rather in "a breed of leaders with sufficient imagination to propose bold yet concrete solutions."[26]

For all his sound proposals, not all of Rorty's interventions hit their mark. His worry that the left's focus on culture caused it to neglect economic class triggered an overreaction where he downplayed the importance of culture. His displeasure with the left's inability to see America's greatness amid its vices made him overcorrect by downplaying the political faults of political figures he admired. For someone who spent so much time critiquing the Cultural Left for not paying enough attention to the economy, Rorty shows almost no awareness in his writings of contemporary debates on alternatives to capitalism, which makes his trademark stance that all-other-economic-systems-have-failed-so-the-best-we-can-hope-for-is-capitalism-with-a-human-face seem surprisingly lazy and dogmatic.

There are other examples of erroneous judgment, tone-deafness, or short-sightedness in his political writings that are likely to be striking for today's reader. However, his insistence upon the need for intellectuals to intervene in the problems of the day with concrete strategies for change, rather than issue, from secure vantages within the ivory tower, detached critiques or self-serving rationalizations of the status quo, is resoundingly relevant. His pragmatic proposals for moral and political reform of our culture and communities speak directly to the most urgent crises of our time. His prophecies about the rise of populism, strongman leaders, a period of Dark Years, and global injustice reach us today as warnings more chilling now than when he wrote. Whether a form of patriotic attachment to America that stops short of nationalism, or an egalitarian, classless, and casteless society, or a "global community of trust" is achievable remain unknowns on which Rorty offers no certainty or even assurances.[27] But he never gave up on the idea that the democratic vista is limited only by our willingness to learn and change.

I

POLITICS AND PHILOSOPHY

1

WHO ARE WE?

MORAL UNIVERSALISM AND ECONOMIC TRIAGE (1996)

In what sort of situation might someone ask the question "Who are we?" It seems most appropriate in the mouth of someone trying to shape her audience into a more coherent community. It is the sort of rhetorical question a party leader might ask at a party rally. In such situations, it means something like "what unifying ideal can we find to make us less like a mob and more like an army, less like people thrown together by accident and more like people who have united to accomplish a task?"

"Who are we?" is quite different from the traditional philosophical question "What are we?" The latter is synonymous with Kant's question, "What is Man?" Both mean something like "how does the human species differ from the rest of the animal kingdom?" or "among the differences between us and the other animals, which ones matter most?" This "what?" question is scientific or metaphysical.

By contrast, the "who?" question is political. It is asked by people who want to separate off the human beings who are better suited to some particular purpose than other human beings, and to gather the former into a self-conscious moral community: that is, a community united by reciprocal trust, and by willingness to come to fellow-members' assistance when they need it. Answers to the "who?" question are attempts to forge, or reforge, a moral identity.

Traditional moral universalism blends an answer to the scientific or metaphysical "what?" question with an answer to the political "who?" question. Universalism presupposes that the discovery of traits shared by all human beings suffices to show why, and perhaps how, all human beings should organize themselves into a cosmopolis. It proposes a scientific or metaphysical foundation for global politics. Following the model of religious claims that human beings are made in the image of God, philosophical universalism claims that the presence of common traits testifies to a common purpose. It says that the form of the ideal human community can be determined by reference to a universal human nature.

The idea of human nature has, in recent Western philosophy, come to seem obsolete. Ever since Darwin, philosophers have become increasingly suspicious of the very idea of naturalness. Western philosophy has been trying to adapt itself to Darwin's claim that what we call biological species are the haphazard productions of chance—a claim which erases the Greek distinction between natural and artificial kinds. For if the paradigm cases of natural kinds—biological species—are accidental results of accidental encounters between mutated genes and environmental niches, then the very idea of naturalness begins to seem artificial. Darwin makes it hard to continue the practice, common to the Greeks and to the Enlightenment, of using the term "natural" as a term of praise.

When the idea of naturalness goes, so does the Greek picture of inquiry as substituting reality for appearance, the way things are in their own intrinsic nature for the various ways human beings find it useful to describe them. The beginnings of the attempt to abandon the reality-appearance distinction are found in Nietzsche's *Twilight of the Idols* and William James's *Pragmatism*. Both books argue that the idea of truth as correspondence to reality only makes sense if reality has an intrinsic nature, and that it is unclear how we could ever tell whether or not a given descriptive vocabulary "corresponds" to such a nature.

The idea that some such vocabularies are somehow closer to the intrinsic nature of reality than others makes sense to religious believers. For those who believe that a certain religion enshrines the Word, and thus the Will, of the Creator and Lord of the Universe, not only does the question "In what language does the universe demand to be described?" make sense, but the answer is already evident. For secularists, however, the only way to make sense of the idea that the universe demands description in a certain vocabulary is to turn to science. Enlightenment secularism suggested that the vocabulary of the natural sciences is nature's own—the divisions made by this vocabulary are the joints at which nature demands to be cut.

James and Nietzsche viewed this sort of scientism as an unfortunate persistence of religious ways of thinking. They urged that the vocabulary of physics is simply one useful vocabulary among others—useful for technological purposes but useless for any others. Both thought that the Enlightenment's attempt to put science in the place of theology was a mistake, as was the initial assumption that the universe somehow *demands* a certain description. Both saw the choice among descriptions as a choice among human purposes, not a choice between human purposes and those of something nonhuman. Their Darwinian view of the human situation persuaded them that descriptions were tools, not attempts to correspond to the nature of reality. Different purposes demand different tools.

Adopting this view means replacing the choice between theological, scientific, and metaphysical descriptions of the world with a choice between human purposes. But the choice of what purposes to have is almost always, in practice, a choice among groups of people rather than a choice among abstract formulae. A choice of purposes to which to devote one's life is typically a choice between actual or possible human communities: between the sort of people who have one overriding purpose and the sort of people who have another. So, on the pragmatist view common to both Nietzsche and James, metaphysical questions are concealed political questions, questions about the group or groups with which one hopes to affiliate oneself, or which one hopes to create.

For example, to adopt a physicalistic metaphysics is to opt for a human community devoted to mastering nature for the sake of what Bacon called "the improvement of man's estate." To reject that metaphysics, either in the terms in which religious fundamentalists would reject it, or in those in which Gandhi or Heidegger would reject it, is to presuppose an alternative answer to the question "Who are we?" Such a rejection is part of an attempt to create a different sort of human community, organized around a different goal.

To sum up what I have been saying so far: I read Nietzsche and James as saying that the question "Who are we?" should replace "What are we?" as the primordial question of philosophy. For it is the one to which we shall always return—the one which has always already been answered when we answer other questions. Every account of what human beings are is, for pragmatists like Nietzsche and James, a disguised proposal for shaping a new human community. The question "Who are we?" replaces the Greek question "What is Being?" and also Kant's questions "What can I know?" and "What is Man?" It replaces all these with a new form of Kant's question "What may I hope?"

In this new form, Kant's question becomes "What may we hope?" For it is no longer, as it was for Kant, a question about the immortality of the individual soul, but about the future of the species. The question "Who are we?" is future oriented in a way in which the question "What are we?" is not. The "what?" question enshrines the pre-Darwinian notion of a human essence, which has its place in a Platonic heaven of other essences. The "who?" question sets aside the notion of essence, of intrinsic reality, and thus, as I have already said, of the distinction between reality and appearance. It thereby stops asking a timeless question, and asks a question about future time. But this question about the future is not a request for a prediction, but rather for a project. To ask who we are becomes a way of asking what future we should try, cooperatively, to build.

Nietzsche and James agree on the primordiality of this question, but disagree about the answer. The two have different projects in mind: Nietzsche's is an aristocratic project and James's democratic. Nietzsche's "we" consists of a happy few, Zarathustra's chosen companions. James's "we" are the inhabitants of a global cooperative commonwealth. James took for granted the universalistic assumption, common to Christianity and the Enlightenment, that our moral community should be identical with our biological species—defined not in any essentialistic way, but simply as consisting of any organism with which any of us can interbreed. This amounts to the project of distributing the planet's resources in such a way that no human child lacks the opportunities for individual development, the life-chances, available to any other human child.

Nietzsche, obviously, did not take this assumption, or this project, for granted. Were he to reappear among us, Nietzsche would presumably say that this project is even more absurd than it was a century before. For now, even if it were desirable, it is obviously unfeasible. In 1900, when there were only one and a half billion people in the world, and there were still forests on land and fish in the sea, such an egalitarian project might have made some sense. But in 2010 we shall have seven billion people, almost no forest, and barely any fish. So, one can imagine Nietzsche saying, even if democratic egalitarianism had been a good idea in 1900, nobody can put it forward as a practical proposal now. Doing so is either hypocritical or self-deceptive.

Nietzsche's point can be restated and enlarged as follows: the part of the world which fostered Christianity and the Enlightenment was exceptionally lucky. The assumption that our moral community should be identical with our biological species, could only have occurred to people who were lucky enough to have more material goods than they really needed. It is not an idea which could have occurred to those who had to struggle to survive. Moral universalism is an invention of the rich.

The rich parts of the world, the ones which have already realized some of the dreams of the Enlightenment, are also the places where technology took off. Technology began making Europe rich even before the Enlightenment began making it democratic. Only people who were already exceptionally rich, and therefore exceptionally secure, could have taken the idea of democracy, much less of global democracy, seriously. Moral idealism goes along with economic success. The latter is obviously not a sufficient condition for the former, but I think we should concede to Nietzsche that it is a necessary one.

I think that we also have to concede to Nietzsche that no foreseeable application of technology could make every human family rich enough to give their children anything remotely like the chances that a family in the lucky parts of the world now takes for granted for theirs. Nobody has written a scenario which ends with every child born in Peru, Angola, and Bangladesh going to school, rather than working, until the age of eighteen, and then, if talented, proceeding to a university for training which will enable it to realize its fullest potentialities. Nobody has even written a scenario showing how a family in these countries would acquire a reason to practice birth control, instead of trying to propagate as many sources of income as possible.

Furthermore, nobody has written a scenario which shows how the people in the lucky industrialized democracies might redistribute their wealth in ways which create bright prospects for the children of the undeveloped countries without destroying the prospects of their own children and of their own societies. The institutions of the rich democracies are now so intertwined with advanced methods of transportation and communication, and more generally with expensive technology, that it is hardly possible to imagine their survival if the rich countries had to reduce their share of the world's resources to a fraction of what they now consume. Democratic institutions in these countries depend on the existence of things like universal literacy, meritocratic social mobility, bureaucratic rationality, and the existence of many competing sources of information about public affairs. Free universities, a free press, incorruptible judges, and unbribable police officers do not come cheap.

To mention all these missing scenarios is to suggest that the rich parts of the world may be in the position of somebody proposing to share her one loaf of bread with a hundred starving people. Even if she does share, everybody, including herself, will starve anyway. So she may easily be guilty, as my hypothetical Nietzsche suggests, either of self-deception or hypocrisy.

I do not know—perhaps nobody knows—whether the project of constructing a global cooperative commonwealth is as hopeless as I have been suggesting it may be. Technology has surprised us before, and so has the success of moral idealists in bringing about the seemingly impossible. Both might surprise us again. Maybe somebody has written scenarios I have not read. But my present concern is not with predictions, either gloomy or optimistic, but rather with describing the present moral situation of the rich and lucky inhabitants of the world in terms of alternative answers to the question "Who are we?"

One way to get these alternatives in focus is to remark that a traditional expression of moral idealism is for a smaller group of people to identify themselves imaginatively with a larger group. Fifty-one years ago, a set of rich and lucky people imagined themselves to be "We, the people of the United Nations." One reason they chose those words was that, a hundred and fifty-six years earlier, some equally rich and lucky people had imagined themselves to be "We, the people of the United States."

It has often been suggested that the authors of the Constitution of the United States of America were not entitled to describe themselves as the people of the United States. They were, it is said, only entitled to call themselves something like "We, the representatives of the property-owning white males of the United States." Their black slaves, their white servants, and even their wives and daughters, did not really come into the picture. Similarly, it has often been suggested that when the representatives of governments signed the Charter of the United Nations, the most that they were really entitled to say was something like "We, the representatives of the political classes of our respective countries."

The existence of a moral community which can plausibly and without qualification identify itself as "We, the people of the United States" is still a project rather than an actuality. In a few respects, my country is closer to accomplishing this project now than it has ever been, thanks to the civil rights revolution of the 1960s and to the continuing pressure exerted by feminists. In most respects, however, it is losing ground. For the gap between rich and poor Americans is widening steadily, and the latter are increasingly bereft of hope for their children's future.

A recent article by Richard Posner, the only American jurist who is also a distinguished and widely known intellectual figure, contains a sentence which underlines this lack of hope. Judge Posner wrote that "the very high crime rate of young black [American] males is an aspect of the pathological situation of the black underclass, but there do not appear to be any remedies for this situation that are at once politically feasible and likely to work."[1] In the context in which Posner writes, "politically feasible" means "compatible with the fact that the American middle class will not let itself be taxed to save the children of the underclass." This unwillingness creates a situation in which those children cannot hope for a decent chance in life. To predict that unwillingness will persist is to say that there will, in the future, no longer be any "we" which unites the political class of the US and those underclass children in a moral community. Those black children are no longer, if Posner's judgment of political feasibility is right, among "we, the people of the United States," any more than their slave ancestors were when the US Constitution was written.

I hope that Posner is wrong, and that the middle class of my own country will not prove to be as cruel and greedy as he predicts. But I have cited Posner on the United States only to pursue the analogy with the United Nations. I think it is important to ask whether it is any longer possible to use the phrase "We, the people of the United Nations" as the name of a moral community, a community which is identical with the human species. The crucial question here is whether it is merely the cruelty and greed of the rich nations which keeps this community from being formed, or whether the formation of such a community is simply impossible, even given all the good will in the world.

Suppose that it is impossible. That is, suppose that there is no imaginable way to make decent life-chances available to the poorer five billion citizens of the member states of the United Nations while still keeping intact the democratic sociopolitical institutions cherished by the richer one billion. Suppose that the hope of such availability is doomed to be either hypocritical or self-deceptive. Suppose that we have passed the point of no return in the balance between population and resources, and that it is now *sauve qui peut*. Suppose that the rich and lucky billion come to believe that this is the case—not out of selfishness and greed, but as a result of accurate economic calculation. Then they will begin to treat the poor and unlucky five billion as surplus to their moral requirements, unable to play a part in their moral life. The rich and lucky people will quickly become unable to think of the poor and unlucky ones as their fellow humans, as part of the same "we."

This may seem overstated. For surely, it might be objected, one can have a sense of identification with people whose suffering one has no way of alleviating. The link between having a sense of community and being able to fulfill obligations to other members of that community—the link between ought and can, between morals and money—is not that tight.

This objection is plausible, but not, I think, convincing. Consider the analogy, suggested by Posner's phrase "pathological situation," between finding it politically unfeasible to give people hope and finding it medically unfeasible to do so. When a hospital is deluged with an impossibly large flood of victims of a catastrophe, the doctors and nurses begin to perform triage: they decide which of the victims are "medically feasible"— which ones are appropriate recipients of the limited medical resources available. When the American underclass is told that it is politically unfeasible to remedy their situation, they are in the same situation as accident victims who are told that it is unfeasible to offer them medical treatment.

In both cases, those who make the decision about feasibility are answering the question "Who are we?" by excluding certain human beings from membership in "We, the ones who can hope to survive." When we realize that it is unfeasible to rescue a person or a group, it is as if they had already gone before us into death. Such people are, as we say, "dead to us." Life, we say, is for the living. For the sake of their own sanity, and for the sake of the less grievously wounded patients who are admitted to the hospital, the doctors and nurses must simply blank out on all those moaning victims who are left outside in the street. They must cease to think about them, and pretend that they are already dead.

These doctors and nurses illustrate the point that if you cannot render assistance to people in need, your claim that they form part of your moral community is empty. This in turn is an illustration of a more general, philosophical point: that it only makes sense to attribute a belief to someone if such an attribution helps one to predict the person's future actions. Beliefs are, as Bain and Peirce said, habits of action. If no actions can be predicted on the basis of a belief-attribution, then the purported belief turns out to be, at most, the mouthing of a formula, a meaningless incantation.

On this Peircean, pragmatic account of belief, to believe that someone is "one of us," a member of our moral community, is to exhibit readiness to come to their assistance when they are in need. To answer the question "Who are we?" in a way that is relevant to moral questions is to pick out whom one is willing to do something to help. Pressing Peirce's point, I would argue that one is answering the question "Who are we?" in a useful and informative way only if one thereby generates reliable predictions about what measures the group identified as "we" will take in specified circumstances.

It follows that it is neither useful nor informative to answer this question by reference to a class of people whom one has no idea how to help. Moral identification is empty when it is no longer tied to habits of action. That is why it is either hypocritical or self-deceptive for the doctors to think of those who are left outside the hospital as "us." It is why it is either hypocritical or self-deceptive for those who agree with Posner about the hopelessness of attempting to rescue the black American underclass from its pathological situation to continue to use a phrase like "We, the people of the United States." It would be equally self-deceptive or hypocritical for those who do not believe that the industrialized democracies can bring either hope or human rights to the billions who lack both to use the term "We, the people of the United Nations."

When the founders of the United States and of the United Nations originally used these terms, however, it was neither self-deceptive nor hypocritical. For the foundation of each of these institutions was part of a project—a project of forming a moral community out of a mass of people which was not yet such a community. Both were founded not only in a spirit of hope, but in the midst of a plethora of practical proposals— proposals which looked, at the time, as if they might be politically and economically feasible. At the time of the foundation of the United Nations, when the world's population was only half its present size and everybody assumed that the forests and the fish would last forever, many proposals seemed politically feasible that seem so no longer.

Perhaps there are feasible political proposals to be made, even today, which would entitle us to use the phrase "We, the people of the United Nations" in a way which is neither empty nor hypocritical. If I knew what they were, I would offer them. But I do not, and so I am making a merely philosophical point.

I can sum up this point as follows: an answer to the question "Who are we?" which is to have any moral significance, has to be one which takes money into account. Marx may have overstated when he identified morality with the interests of an economic class, but he had a point. That point is that a politically feasible project of egalitarian redistribution of wealth requires there to be enough money around to ensure that, after the redistribution, the rich will still be able to recognize themselves—will still think their lives worth living. The only way in which the rich can think of themselves as part of the same moral community with the poor is by reference to some scenario which gives hope to the children of the poor without depriving their own children of hope.

As I said earlier, I am not trying to make predictions. Nor am I offering recommendations for action. Rather, I have been putting forward a philosophical argument that depends upon three premises. The first is that the primordial philosophical question is not "What are we?" but "Who are we?" The second is that "who are we?" means "what community of reciprocal trust do we belong to?" The third is that reciprocal trust depends on feasibility as well as on good will. The conclusion I draw from these premises is that thinking of other people as part of the same "we," depends not only on willingness to help those people but on belief that one is able to help them. In particular, answering the question "Who are we?" with "we are members of a moral community which encompasses the human species," depends on an ability to believe that we can avoid economic triage.

2

DEMOCRACY AND PHILOSOPHY

(2007)

Philosophy is a ladder that Western political thinking climbed up, and then shoved aside. Starting in the seventeenth century, philosophy played an important role in clearing the way for the establishment of democratic institutions in the West. It did so by secularizing political thinking—substituting questions about how human beings could lead happier lives for questions about how God's will might be done. Philosophers suggested that people should just put religious revelation to one side, at least for political purposes, and act as if human beings were on their own—free to shape their own laws and their own institutions to suit their felt needs, free to make a fresh start.

In the eighteenth century, during the European Enlightenment, differences between political institutions, and movements of political opinion, reflected different philosophical views. Those sympathetic to the old regime were less likely to be materialistic atheists than were the people who wanted revolutionary social change. But now that Enlightenment values are pretty much taken for granted throughout the West, this is no longer the case. Nowadays politics leads the way, and philosophy tags along behind. One first decides on a political outlook and then, if one has a taste for that sort of thing, looks for philosophical backup. But such a taste is optional, and rather uncommon. Most Western intellectuals know little about philosophy, and care still less. In their eyes, thinking that political proposals reflect philosophical convictions is like thinking that the tail wags the dog.

I shall be developing this theme of the irrelevance of philosophy to democracy in my remarks. Most of what I shall say will be about the situation in my own country, but I think that most of it applies equally well to the European democracies. In those countries, as in the US, the word "democracy" has gradually come to have two distinct meanings. In its narrower, minimalist, meaning, it refers to a system of government in which power is in the hands of freely elected officials. I shall call democracy in this sense "constitutionalism." In its wider sense, it refers to a social ideal, that of equality of opportunity. In this second sense, a democracy is a society in which all children have the same chances in life, and in which nobody suffers from being born poor, or being the descendant of slaves, or being female, or being homosexual. I shall call democracy in this sense "egalitarianism."

Suppose that, at the time of the US presidential election of 2004, you had asked voters who were wholeheartedly in favor of reelecting President Bush whether they believed in democracy. They would have been astonished by the question, and have replied that of course they did. But all they would have meant by this is that they believe in constitutional government. Because of this belief, they were prepared to accept the outcome of the election, whatever it turned out to be. If Kerry had won, they would be angry and disgusted. But they would not have dreamt of trying to prevent his taking office by going out into the streets. They would have been utterly horrified by the suggestion that the generals in the Pentagon should mount a military coup in order to keep Bush in the White House.

The voters who in 2004 regarded Bush as the worst American president of modern times, and who desperately hoped for Kerry's success were also constitutionalists. When Kerry lost, they were sick at heart. But they did not dream of fomenting a revolution. Left-wing Democrats are as committed to preserving the US Constitution as are right-wing Republicans.

But if, instead of asking these two groups whether they believe in democracy, you had asked them what they mean by the term "democracy," you might have gotten different replies. The Bush voters will usually be content to define democracy simply as government by freely elected officials. But many of the Kerry voters—and especially the intellectuals—will say that America—despite centuries of free elections and the gradual expansion of the franchise to include all adult citizens—is not yet a full-fledged democracy. Their point is that although it obviously is a democracy in the constitutional sense, it is not yet a democracy in the egalitarian sense. For equality of opportunity has not yet been attained. The gap between the rich and the poor is widening rather than narrowing. Power is becoming more concentrated in the hands of the few.

These left-wing Democrats will remind you of the likely fate of the children of badly educated Americans, both black and white, raised in a home in which the full-time labor of both mother and father brings in only about $40,000 a year. This sounds like a lot of money, but in America children of parents at that income level are deprived of many advantages, will probably be unable to go to college, and will be unlikely to get a good job. For Americans who think of themselves as on the political left, these inequalities are outrageous. They demonstrate that even though America has a democratically elected government, it still does not have a democratic society.

Ever since Walt Whitman wrote his essay "Democratic Vistas" in the middle of the nineteenth century, a substantial sector of educated public opinion in the US has used "democracy" to mean "social egalitarianism" rather than simply "representative government." Using the term in this way became common in the Progressive Era and still more common under the New Deal. That usage permitted the civil rights movement led by Martin Luther King Jr., the feminist movement, and the gay and lesbian rights movement to portray themselves as successive attempts to "realize the promise of American democracy."

So far I have said nothing about the relation of religion to American democracy. But for an understanding of the ongoing contest between constitutionalist and egalitarian understandings of democracy, it is important to realize that Americans on the political left tend to be less religiously committed and religiously active than people on the political right. The leftists who are religious believers do not try very hard to bring their religious convictions and their political preferences together. They treat religion as a private matter, endorse the Jeffersonian tradition of religious tolerance, and are emphatic in their preference for the strict separation of church and state.

On the political right, however, religious and political convictions are often interwoven. The hard-core Bush voters are not only considerably more likely to go to church than the hard-core Kerry voters, but are considerably more likely to sympathize with Bush's insistence on the need to elect officials who take God seriously. They often describe the United States of America as a nation especially blessed by the Christian God. They like to say that theirs is "a Christian country," and do not realize that this phrase is offensive to their Jewish and Muslim fellow citizens. They tend to see America's emergence as the only superpower left standing not just as an accident of history, but as evidence of divine favor.

Because of this different stance toward religious belief, one might be tempted to think of the opposition between the political right and the political left as reflecting a difference between those who think of democracy as built upon religious foundations and those who think of it as built upon philosophical foundations. But, as I have already suggested, that would be misleading. Except for a few professors of theology and philosophy, neither rightist nor leftist American intellectuals think of democracy in the sense of constitutionalism as having *either* sort of foundation.

If asked to justify their preference for constitutional government, both sides would be more likely to appeal to historical experience rather than to either religious or philosophical principles. Both would be likely to endorse Winston Churchill's much-quoted remark that "democracy is the worst form of government except for all those other forms which have been tried from time to time." Both agree that a free press, a free judiciary, and free elections are the best safeguard against the abuse of governmental power characteristic of the old European monarchies, and of fascist and communist regimes.

The arguments between leftists and rightists about the need for egalitarian social legislation are also matters neither of opposing religious beliefs nor of opposing philosophical principles. The disagreement between those who think of a commitment to democracy as a commitment to an egalitarian society and those who have no use for the welfare state and for government regulations designed to ensure equality of opportunity is not fought out on either philosophical or religious grounds. Even the most fanatic fundamentalists do not try to argue that the Christian Scriptures provide reasons why the American government should not redistribute wealth by using taxpayers' money to send the children of the poor to college. Their leftist opponents do not claim that the need to use taxpayer's money for this purpose is somehow dictated by what Kant called "the tribunal of pure reason."

Typically the arguments between the two camps are much more pragmatic. The right claims that imposing high taxes in order to benefit the poor will lead to "big government," rule by bureaucrats, and a sluggish economy. The left concedes that there is a danger of overbureaucratization and of overcentralized government. But, they argue, these dangers are outweighed by the need to make up for the injustices built into a capitalist economy—a system that can throw thousands of people out of work overnight and make it impossible for them to feed, much less educate, their children. The right argues that the left is too much inclined to imposing its own tastes on society as a whole. The left replies that what the right calls a "matter of taste" is really a matter of justice.

Such arguments proceed not by appeals to universally valid moral obligations but by appeals to historical experience—the experience of overregulation and overtaxation on the one hand and the experience of poverty and humiliation on the other. The rightists accuse the leftists of being sentimental fools— bleeding-heart liberals—who do not understand the need to keep government small so that individual freedom can flourish. The leftists accuse the rightists of heartlessness—of being unable or unwilling to imagine themselves in the situation of a parent who cannot make enough money to clothe his daughter as well as her schoolmates are clothed. Such polemical exchanges are pursued at a pragmatic level, and no theological or philosophical sophistication is required to conduct them. Nor would such sophistication do much to strengthen either side.

So far I have been talking about the form that contemporary American political disagreements take, and emphasizing the irrelevance of philosophy to such disputes. I have been arguing that neither the agreement between the left and the right on the wisdom of retaining constitutional government nor the disagreement between them about what laws to pass has much to do with either religious conviction or philosophical opinion. You can be a very intelligent and useful participant in political discussion in contemporary democratic societies such as the US even though you have no interest whatever in either religion or philosophy.

Despite this fact, one still occasionally comes across debates among philosophers about whether democracy has "philosophical foundations," and about what these might be. I do not regard these debates as very useful. To understand why they are still conducted, it helps to remember the point I made at the outset: that when the democratic revolutions of the eighteenth century broke out, the quarrel between religion and philosophy had an importance it now lacks. For those revolutions were not able to appeal to the past. They could not point to the successes enjoyed by democratic and secularist regimes. For few such regimes had ever existed, and those that had had not always fared well. So their only recourse was to justify themselves by reference to principle, philosophical principle. Reason, they said, had revealed the existence of universal human rights, so a revolution was required to put society on a rational basis.

"Reason" in the eighteenth century was supposed to be what the anticlericalists had to compensate for their lack of what the clergy called "faith." For the revolutionaries of those times were necessarily anticlerical. One of their chief complaints was the assistance that the clergy had rendered to feudal and monarchical institutions. Diderot, for example, famously looked forward to seeing the last king strangled with the entrails of the last priest. In that period, the work of secularist philosophers such as Spinoza and Kant was very important in creating an intellectual climate conducive to revolutionary political activity. Kant argued that even the words of Christ must be evaluated by reference to the dictates of universally shared human reason. For Enlightenment thinkers such as Jefferson, it was important to argue that reason is a sufficient basis for moral and political deliberation, and that revelation is unnecessary.

The author of both the Virginia Statute of Religious Freedom and of the American Declaration of Independence, Jefferson was a typical leftist intellectual of his time. He read a lot of philosophy and took it very seriously indeed. He wrote in the Declaration that "We hold these truths to be self-evident: that all men are created equal, that they are endowed by their creator with certain inalienable rights, that among them are life, liberty and the pursuit of happiness." As a good Enlightenment rationalist, he agreed with Kant that reason was the source of such truths, and that reason was sufficient to provide moral and political guidance.

Many contemporary Western intellectuals (among them Jürgen Habermas, the most influential and distinguished living philosopher) think that there was something importantly right about Enlightenment rationalism. Habermas believes that philosophical reflection can indeed provide moral and political guidance, for it can disclose principles that have what he calls "universal validity." Foundationalist philosophers like Habermas see philosophy as playing the same role in culture that Kant and Jefferson assigned to it. Simply taking thought will reveal what Habermas calls "presuppositions of rational communication," and thereby provide criteria which can guide moral and political choice.

Many leftist intellectuals in America and in the West generally would agree that democracy has such a foundation. They too think that certain central moral and political truths are, if not exactly self-evident, nonetheless transcultural and ahistorical—the product of human reason as such, not simply of a certain sequence of historical events. They are annoyed and disturbed by the writings of antifoundationalist philosophers like myself who argue that there is no such thing as "human reason."

We antifoundationalists, however, regard Enlightenment rationalism as an unfortunate attempt to beat religion at religion's own game—the game of pretending that there is something above and beyond human history that can sit in judgment on that history. We argue that although some cultures are better than others, there are no transcultural criteria of "betterness" that we can appeal to when we say that modern democratic societies are better than feudal societies, or that egalitarian societies are better than racist or sexist ones. We are sure that rule by officials freely elected by literate and well-educated voters is better than rule by priests and kings, but we would not try to demonstrate the truth of this claim to a proponent of theocracy or of monarchy. We suspect that if the study of history cannot convince such a proponent of the falsity of his views, nothing else can do so.

Antifoundationalist philosophy professors like myself do not think that philosophy is as important as Plato and Kant thought it. This is because we do not think that the moral world has a structure that can be discerned by philosophical reflection. We are historicists because we agree with Hegel's thesis that "philosophy is its time held in thought." What Hegel meant, I take it, was that human social practices in general, and political institutions in particular, are the product of concrete historical situations, and that they have to be judged by reference to the needs created by those situations. There is no way to step outside of human history and look at things under the aspect of eternity.

Philosophy, on this view, is ancillary to historiography. The history of philosophy should be studied in the context of the social situations that created philosophical doctrines and systems, in the same way that we study the history of art and literature. Philosophy is not, and never will be, a science—in the sense of a progressive accumulation of enduring truths.

Most philosophers in the West prior to the time of Hegel were universalist and foundationalist. As Isaiah Berlin has put it, before the end of the eighteenth century, Western thinkers viewed human life as the attempt to solve a jigsaw puzzle. Berlin describes what I have portrayed as their hope for universal philosophical foundations for culture as follows:

> There must be some way of putting the pieces together. The all-wise being, the omniscient being, whether God or an omniscient earthly creature—whichever way you like to conceive of it—is in principle capable of fitting all the pieces together into one coherent pattern. Anyone who does this will know what the world is like: what things are, what they have been, what they will be, what the laws are that govern them, what man is, what the relation of man is to things, and therefore what man needs, what he desires, and how to obtain it.[1]

The idea that the intellectual world, including the moral world, is like a jigsaw puzzle, and that philosophers are the people charged with getting all the pieces to fit together, presupposes that history does not really matter: that there has never been anything new under the sun. That assumption was weakened by three events. The first was the spate of democratic revolutions at the end of the eighteenth century, especially those in America and in France. The second was the Romantic Movement in literature and the arts—a movement that suggested that the poet, rather than the philosopher, was the figure who had most to contribute to social progress. The third, which came along a little later, was the general acceptance of Darwin's evolutionary account of the origin of the human species.

One of the effects of these three events was the emergence of antifoundationalist philosophy—of philosophers who challenge the jigsaw puzzle view of things. The Western philosophical tradition, these philosophers say, was wrong to think that the enduring and stable was preferable to the novel and contingent. Plato, in particular, was wrong to take mathematics as a model for knowledge.

On this view, there is no such thing as human nature, for human beings make themselves up as they go along. They create themselves, as poets create poems. There is no such thing as the nature of the state or the nature of society to be understood— there is only a historical sequence of relatively successful and relatively unsuccessful attempts to achieve some combination of order and justice.

To further illustrate the difference between foundationalists and antifoundationalists, let me return to Jefferson's claim that the rights to life, liberty, and the pursuit of happiness are self-evident. Foundationalists urge that the existence of such rights is a universal truth, one that has nothing in particular to do with Europe rather than Asia or Africa, or with modern history rather than ancient history. The existence of such rights, they say, is like the existence of irrational numbers such as the square root of two—something that anybody who thinks hard about the topic can be brought to recognize. Such philosophers agree with Kant's claim that "the common moral consciousness" is not a historical product but part of the structure of human rationality. Kant's categorical imperative, dictating that we must not use other human beings as mere means—must not treat them as mere things—is translated into concrete political terms by Jefferson and by the authors of the Helsinki Declaration of Human Rights. Such translations simply reformulate moral convictions that should have seemed as self-evidently true in the days of Plato and Alexander as they are now. It is the business of philosophy to remind us of what, somehow, deep in our hearts, we have always known to be true. Plato was, in this sense, right when he said that moral knowledge is a matter of recollection— an a priori matter, not a result of empirical experimentation.

In contrast, antifoundationalists like myself agree with Hegel that Kant's categorical imperative is an empty abstraction until it is filled up with the sort of concrete detail that only historical experience can provide. We say the same about Jefferson's claim about self-evident human rights. On our view, moral principles are never more than ways of summing up a certain body of experience. To call them "a priori" or "self-evident" is to persist in using Plato's utterly misleading analogy between moral certainty and mathematical certainty. No statements can both have revolutionary political implications and be self-evidently true.

To say that a statement is self-evident is, we antifoundationalists believe, merely an empty rhetorical gesture. The existence of the rights that the revolutionaries of the eighteenth century claimed for all human beings had not been evident to most European thinkers in the previous thousand years. That their existence seems self-evident to Americans and Europeans two hundred-odd years after they were first asserted is to be explained by culture-specific indoctrination rather than by a sort of connaturality between the human mind and moral truth.

To make our case, we antifoundationalists point to unpleasant historical facts such as the following: The words of the Declaration were taken, by the supposedly democratic government of the US, to apply only to people of European origin. The American Founding Fathers applied them only to the immigrants who had come across the Atlantic to escape from the monarchical governments of Europe. The idea that native Americans—the Indian tribes who were the aboriginal inhabitants—had such rights was rarely taken seriously. Recalcitrant Indians were massacred.

Again, it was only a hundred years after the Declaration of Independence that the citizenry of the US began to take women's rights seriously—began to ask themselves whether American females were being given the same opportunities for the pursuit of happiness as were American males. It took almost a hundred years, and an enormously costly and cruel civil war, before black Americans were given the right not to be held as slaves. It took another hundred years before black Americans began to be treated as full-fledged citizens, entitled to all the same opportunities as whites.

These facts of the history of my country are sometimes cited to show that America is an utterly hypocritical nation, and that it has never taken seriously its own protestations about human rights. But I think that this dismissal of the US is unfair and misleading. One reason it became a much better, fairer, more decent, more generous country in the course of two centuries was that democratic freedoms—in particular freedom of the press and freedom of speech—made it possible for public opinion to force the white males of European ancestry to consider what they had done, and were doing to the Indians, the women, and the blacks.

The role of public opinion in the gradual expansion of the scope of human rights in the Western democracies is, to my mind, the best reason for preferring democracy to other systems of government that one could possibly offer. The history of the US illustrates the way in which a society that concerned itself largely with the happiness of property-owning white males could gradually and peacefully change itself into one in which impoverished black females have become senators, cabinet officers, and judges of the higher courts. Jefferson and Kant would have been bewildered at the changes that have taken place in the Western democracies in the last two hundred years. For they did not think of equal treatment for blacks and whites, or of female suffrage, as deducible from the philosophical principles they enunciated. Their astonishment illustrates the antifoundationalist point that moral insight is not, like mathematics, a product of rational reflection. It is instead a matter of imagining a better future, and observing the results of attempts to bring that future into existence. Moral knowledge, like scientific knowledge, is mostly the result of making experiments and seeing how they work out. Female suffrage, for example, has worked well. Centralized control of a country's economy, on the other hand, has not.

The history of moral progress since the Enlightenment illustrates the fact that the important thing about democracy is as much a matter of freedom of speech and of the press as about the ability of angry citizens to replace bad elected officials with better elected officials. A country can have democratic elections but make no moral progress if those who are being mistreated have no chance to make their sufferings known. In theory, a country could remain a constitutional democracy even if its government never instituted any measures to increase equality of opportunity. In practice, the freedom to debate political issues and to put forward political candidates will ensure that democracy in the sense of egalitarianism will be a natural consequence of democracy as constitutional government.

The moral of the antifoundationalist sermon I have been preaching to you is that for countries that have not undergone the secularization that was the most important effect of the European Enlightenment, or that are only now seeing the emergence of constitutional government, the history of Western philosophy is not a particularly profitable area of study. The history of the successes and failures of various social experiments in various countries is much more profitable. If we antifoundationalists are right, the attempt to place society on a philosophical foundation should be replaced by the attempt to learn from the historical record.

3

DEWEY AND POSNER ON PRAGMATISM
AND MORAL PROGRESS

(2007)

I was greatly honored to be asked to give the Dewey Lecture, and very happy to have an occasion to revisit my old university. I entered the so-called Hutchins College in 1946, and left the University of Chicago with an MA in philosophy six years later. Those were the richest and most stimulating years of my intellectual life.

When I came to Chicago, John Dewey was still alive, but his influence had waned. In those days, the best students in the University were sitting at the feet of Leo Strauss, who taught them that Plato had been magnificently right and Dewey dangerously wrong. "Utility and truth," Strauss wrote, "are two entirely different things."[1]

In recent decades, pragmatism has made a comeback. Judge Richard Posner has been one of the leaders of this revival. I have learned a great deal from Judge Posner's books, and share his overall philosophical outlook. But we still disagree on certain issues. I shall argue in this lecture that on one of those issues—the question of whether the modern West has made moral progress—Dewey would have been on my side.

———

Strauss was not the first German to be dismissive about pragmatism. Georg Simmel described it as "what the Americans were able to get out of [Friedrich] Nietzsche."[2] Simmel was wrong if he thought that William James and Dewey got their ideas from Nietzsche, but he was right that their views overlapped his. All three wanted us to stop asking metaphysical questions about the nature of reality and about the nature of human beings. But James and Dewey were better than Nietzsche at formulating a coherent antimetaphysical outlook.

Nietzsche is notorious for his vacillations. He wavers between criticizing the very idea of objective truth and proclaiming that his own views are objectively true and everybody else's objectively false. On one page he tells us that "we simply lack any organ for knowledge, for 'truth': we 'know' (or believe or imagine) just as much as may be *useful* in the interests of the human herd, the species."[3] But a few pages earlier he had said that "even we . . . godless anti-metaphysicians still take our fire, too, from the flame lit by a faith that is thousands of years old . . . the faith of Plato . . . that truth is divine."[4]

At his best, however, Nietzsche explicitly rejected the science-worship that still links much of twenty-first-century analytic philosophy to nineteenth-century positivism. When he says "there are no facts, only interpretations,"[5] and seems willing to admit that this goes for his own assertions as well, he edges closer to the more coherent position that James and Dewey adopted. Both of these philosophers would have agreed with Nietzsche that "a 'scientific' interpretation of the world . . . might therefore still be one of the *most stupid* of all possible interpretations . . . one of the poorest in meaning."[6] Unfortunately, however, passages like that one are offset by Nietzsche's bursts of positivistic braggadocio, as when he writes, "long live physics! And even more so that which *compels* us to turn to physics—our honesty!"[7]

The American pragmatists did consistently what Nietzsche did only occasionally and halfheartedly: they abandoned positivism's attempt to elevate science above the rest of culture. They treated the quarrel between Platonic immaterialism and Democritean materialism, as well as all other metaphysical disputes, as irrelevant to practice and thus not worth discussing. Pragmatists substitute the question "which descriptions of the human situation are most useful for which human purposes?" for the question "which description tells us what that situation really is?" Pragmatism puts natural science on all fours with politics and art. It is one more source of suggestions about what to do with our lives. We might, for example, colonize the planets of other stars. Or we might tweak our genes, in order to give birth to *Übermenschen*. Or we might try to equalize the life-chances of rich children and poor children. Or we might try to make our individual lives into works of art. Dewey thought that we should not try to ground our choices among alternatives such as these on knowledge of what human beings "really" are. For, as he put it, the term "'reality' is a term of value or choice."[8] Philosophy, he insisted, "is [not] in any sense whatever a form of knowledge." It is, instead, "a social hope reduced to a working program of action, a prophecy of the future."[9]

If you agree with Dewey, as I do, about what philosophy is good for, you will see much of contemporary philosophy as a struggle between the heirs of Immanuel Kant and the heirs of

G. W. F. Hegel. Present-day neo-Kantians persist in trying to make philosophy into a branch of knowledge. Contemporary neo-Hegelians hope to grasp the present moment in thought, in order to formulate better prophecies of better futures. Dewey praised Hegel for having recognized that "the moral consciousness of the individual is but a phase in the process of social organization."[10] His own way of doing moral philosophy was to compare alternative programs of action, and alternative prophecies.

Dewey's legacy is, of course, ambiguous. There is considerable disagreement among his admirers about what programs of action follow from his pragmatism. Cheryl Misak and Robert Westbrook, for example, claim that Dewey inferred from a pragmatist view of knowledge to the need for deliberative democracy.[11] Westbrook argues both that "pragmatist epistemology alone is enough to provide grounds for criticism of those who refuse to open their beliefs to the widest possible range of experience and inquiry,"[12] and that deliberative democracy is the only form of government that can provide such openness.[13]

As Westbrook ruefully remarks, "No pragmatist has worked harder to break the link between pragmatism and deliberative democracy than Richard Posner."[14] I agree with Posner when he says that "the bridge [Dewey] tried to build between epistemic and political democracy is too flimsy to carry heavy traffic."[15] Dewey's attempts to build that bridge were, I think, half-hearted and spasmodic. As long as he defined democracy merely as "a name for a life of free and enriching communion,"[16] it was easy for him to argue that the cause of democracy would be furthered if we abandoned both metaphysics and the correspondence theory of truth. But one can praise such a life without believing that the masses should have a larger role in forming public policy. One can agree wholeheartedly with Dewey about the nature of truth, knowledge, and inquiry, and nevertheless agree with Posner that what he calls "our present system of elective aristocracy" is the best we can do.

But though Posner and I agree on this matter, we disagree about another issue. As good neo-Hegelians, we both view the moral consciousness of the individual as a matter of internalized social norms. I think that our norms are better than those of our ancestors. Posner, however, rejects the idea that we have made moral progress. I see this rejection as a relapse from the true pragmatist faith into positivistic science-worship.

———

Toward the beginning of his book, *The Problematics of Moral and Legal Theory*, Posner defines "morality" as "the set of duties to others . . . that are supposed to check our merely self-interested, emotional, or sentimental reactions to serious questions of human conduct."[17] He goes on to say that "the genuineness of morality as a system of social control is not in question."[18] But since systems of social control are obviously local, he argues, so are moralities.

Posner admits, "There are a handful of rudimentary principles of social cooperation—such as don't lie *all* the time . . . that may be common to all human societies."[19] But these, he says, "are too abstract to be criterial."[20] To get guides to action, genuine checks to self-interest, you need thicker notions than those used to state these abstract principles. As Posner says, "What counts [for example] as murder, or as bribery, varies enormously from society to society."[21] So, he continues, "meaningful moral realism is therefore out, and a form . . . of moral relativism is in."[22] Furthermore, "moral principles that claim universality can usually be better understood as just the fancy dress of workaday social norms that vary from society to society."[23]

Up to this point, Posner and Dewey are pretty much in accord. Dewey's early reaction against both John Calvin and Kant left him very suspicious of universal moral principles. He says, for example, "Ready-made rules available at a moment's notice for settling any kind of moral difficulty . . . have been the chief object of the ambition of moralists. In the much less complicated and less changing matters of bodily health such pretensions are known as quackery."[24]

One searches in vain through Dewey's work for the sort of abstract principles offered by Kant, John Stuart Mill, John Rawls, and Jürgen Habermas, and indeed for anything that can happily be described as "a moral theory." Dewey might well have agreed with Posner that "academic moralism is incapable of contributing significantly to the resolution of moral or legal issues."[25]

But it is less clear that Dewey would have inferred, as Posner does, from moral realism being out to moral relativism being in. It depends, obviously, on what you mean by "moral relativism." If you mean merely that, as Posner puts it, "our modern beliefs concerning cruelty and inequality are contingent, rather than being the emanations of a universal law,"[26] then both Hegel and Dewey will count as relativists. So, for that matter, will Rawls. For in this sense moral relativism is merely the denial that knowledge of something transcultural—something like the will of God or the dictates of pure practical reason—can help us decide between competing systems of social control. But when Posner goes on to say that "it is provincial to say that 'we are right about slavery, for example, and the Greeks wrong,'"[27] I think Dewey would demur. He would be startled by Posner's claim that "the relativity of morals implies that there is no moral progress in any sense flattering to the residents of wealthy modern nations."[28]

I think Dewey would respond to Posner by saying:

Of course our judgment of our own rightness is provincial. So are all our judgments about anything. But why should the fact that we use the criteria of our time and place to judge that we have made progress cast doubt on that judgment? What other criteria are available? If you mean simply that only nations as rich and lucky as those of the modern West can get along without slaves, you have a point. But why deny that our wealth and good fortune have enabled us to become morally better?

Dewey thought that the contingency of our moral outlook, and its dependence on material conditions, no more impugns our moral superiority than Galileo's dependence on expensive new optical technology impugned the Copernican theory of the heavens. We can no more help thinking of ourselves as morally superior to our ancestors than we can help believing modern astrophysics to be better than Aristotle's. Mock-modesty about either intellectual or moral progress is an example of what Charles S. Peirce called "make-believe doubt"[29]—doubt that has no effect on practice.

The line of argument I am attributing to Dewey marks the point at which pragmatism and positivism diverge. Pragmatists of my persuasion spend a lot of time doing what Posner disparagingly describes as a "level[ing] down" of science.[30] We do this so that science will no longer seem to tower over morality. Posner says of this strategy that it "may succeed in equating scientific to moral inquiry at the semantic level, but it leaves untouched the vast practical difference in the success of these enterprises."[31] I do not see any such difference. We in the modern West know much more about right and wrong than we did two centuries ago, just as we know much more about how nature works. We have been equally successful in both morals and physics. To be sure, we have more difficulty convincing people of our moral views than of our scientific views, but this does not mean that the two differ in something called "epistemic status."

I reject the notion of epistemic status because, like Thomas Kuhn and Dewey, I see scientific inquiry as working in much the same way as does moral and political inquiry. Posner, like the positivists, sees a big difference. When Posner argues that moral philosophy is "epistemically feeble"[32] on the ground that "the criteria for pronouncing a moral claim valid are given by the culture in which the claim is advanced,"[33] Kuhnians like myself reply that the same argument would show the epistemic feebleness of physics and biology.

In response to this line of argument, Posner says,

> Even if scientific realism is rejected in favor of the view that science yields "objective" results only because scientists happen to form a cohesive, like-minded community—even if, that is, we accept the view that consensus is the only basis on which truth claims can or should be accepted because consensus makes "truth" rather than truth forcing consensus— moral theorists are up against the brute fact that there is no consensus with regard to moral principles from which answers to contested moral questions might actually be derived.[34]

Posner is claiming that, even if we give up the idea of "truth forcing consensus," a crucial difference between science and morals remains. I would make two points in reply. First, brute facts about the presence or absence of consensus—whether about planetary orbits or about sodomy—are to be explained sociologically rather than epistemologically. To explain absence of consensus by "lack of cognitive status" is like explaining a substance's failure to put you to sleep by its lack of dormitive power.

Second, it does not matter whether we can get consensus on moral principles as long as we can get it on practices. As I said earlier, I agree with both Posner and Dewey that moral philosophy will never come up with analogues of Newton's laws—principles that bear on particular cases in the straightforward and uncontroversial way in which physical theory bears on particular observable events. But that asymmetry between physics and morality does nothing to impugn the existence of moral progress. Our practices have changed for the better, even if philosophers cannot agree on what principles "ground" these improved practices.

Posner has remarked that even Justice Scalia would now adjudge the lash and the stocks to be cruel and unusual punishments, even though they were not so regarded by those who drafted the Eighth Amendment. Most of us, and probably Scalia as well, would agree that this change constitutes moral progress. One can agree with Posner that moral philosophy is of no help in providing the courts with reasons for enjoining the use of the lash. But that is no reason to deny that our judges have, like the rest of us, become better able to tell cruelty when they see it. They do not need to be able to define it.

The advantage of pragmatism over positivism is that pragmatists have no trouble with the idea that propositions such as "the stocks and the lash are cruel punishments" and "there is nothing immoral about sodomy" have recently been discovered to be true. They are true, on a pragmatist view, in just the same way that it is true that $E = mc^2$. The fact that moralities are, among other things, local systems of social control does no more to cast doubts on moral progress than the fact that scientific breakthroughs are financed by people hoping for improved technology casts on progress in the "hard" sciences.

A willingness to level down science in this way is, as I see it, the biggest difference between pragmatism and positivism. Kuhn was one of the best things that ever happened to pragmatism, for his work helped us accept Dewey's suggestion that reasoning in morals is no different from reasoning in science—a suggestion Posner explicitly rejects. As I see it, Kuhn demythologized scientific theory-choice in the same way that Posner has demythologized judicial decision-making.

————

Admittedly, however, leveling-down of this sort still looks fishy both to common sense and to the majority of analytic philosophers. This is because both are still tempted to say that if a sentence is true, there must be something that *makes* it true. The physical world, they continue, makes Newton's laws true, but it is not clear what makes moral judgments true. So, the argument goes, perhaps the only value judgments that can be thought of as true are empirical predictions about what means will best serve which ends. Posner seems to buy in on this line of thought. He is quick to argue from what he calls "our inability to reason about ends" to the conclusion that there is no such thing as better apprehension of moral truth.

But pragmatists, at least those of my sect, do not think that anything—either the physical world or the consensus of inquirers—*makes* beliefs true. We have as little use for the notion of "what makes a true sentence true" as we do for that of "what a true sentence corresponds to." On our view, all consensus does is help us *recognize* moral truths. We can cheerfully agree that truths—all kinds of truths—are eternal and absolute. It was true before the foundations of the world were laid both that $2 + 2 = 4$ and that I should be wearing this particular tie today. It was also true that the lash is, in the sense of the Eighth Amendment, a cruel punishment. Eternal and absolute truth is the only kind of truth there is, even though the only way we know what is true is by reaching a consensus that may well prove transitory. All that can be salvaged from the claim that truth is a product of consensus is that finding out what other people believe is, most of the time, a good way to decide what to believe oneself.

But only most of the time. If consensus were all we ever had to go on, there would never have been either scientific or moral progress. We should have had neither Galilean mechanics nor the civil rights movement. One of the features of science that Kuhn helped us appreciate is that great leaps forward occur only when some imaginative genius puts a new interpretation on familiar facts. Percy Bysshe Shelley's *Defense of Poetry* helped us realize that the same thing is true of morality. As he put it, "Reason is to Imagination as the instrument to the agent, as the body to the spirit, as the shadow to the substance."[35]

Dewey endorsed this analogy, as well as Shelley's claim that "the great instrument of moral good is the imagination; and poetry administers to the effect by acting upon the cause."[36] He agreed with Shelley that "ethical science arranges the elements which poetry has created."[37] Only the imagination can break through the crust of convention. Galileo did for Aristotle's hylomorphic physics what Martin Luther King Jr. did for the Southern Way of Life. He dreamed up an alternative. The attractiveness of that alternative gradually undermined an old consensus and built up a new one.

Posner's label for people like King and Catharine MacKinnon is "moral entrepreneur."[38] He is quite ready to acknowledge that if it were not for people like these, we should still be sentencing

criminals to the lash, segregating the water fountains, and enforcing the antisodomy laws. But his positivistic leanings are apparent
from his description of how these entrepreneurs do their work. Of
MacKinnon he writes, "Her influential version of radical feminism
is not offered without supporting arguments. But her influence is
not due to the quality of those arguments. It is due to her polemical skills, her singlemindedness, [and] her passion."[39] "Moral
entrepreneurs," Posner tells us, "persuade, but not with rational
arguments."[40] They use "techniques of nonrational persuasion."[41]

Posner's positivism takes another form when he tries to explain the success of such entrepreneurs by saying that they are
"like arbitrageurs in the securities markets. . . . They spot the
discrepancy between the existing code and the changing environment and persuade the society to adopt a new, more adaptive,
code."[42] I think that Dewey would have found Posner's analogy
with the arbitrageur misleading, and perhaps a bit repellent.
Posner (like his fellow economics fan, Karl Marx) is distrustful
of moral idealism. Dewey wallowed in it.

If we adopt Shelley's and Dewey's account of moral progress,
we shall think of Martin Luther King, Betty Friedan, and the
leaders of the gay rights movement as helping to create, rather
than as detecting, a changed environment. They changed it by
telling us, single-mindedly and passionately, how human lives
were being needlessly damaged by cruel institutions. They incited social hope by proposing programs of action, and by
prophesying a better future. These so-called nonrational methods worked. Posner's notion of "adaptation" seems to me of no
use when we try to explain why they worked.

Posner has set things up so that moral idealists cannot look
good. For if they try to avoid nonrational persuasion by appealing to abstract principle, he (like Stanley Fish) will point out
that they are ignoring Ludwig Wittgenstein's point that no rule

can determine its own interpretation. Yet if the romantic idealists refrain from citing such principles, Posner will tell them that they have abandoned rational argumentation in favor of other, more dubious, polemical tactics.

Posner draws an invidious contrast between heroic figures like Mill and Nietzsche, whom he admires, and such "modern moral philosophers" as Rawls, Ronald Dworkin, Joseph Raz, and T. M. Scanlon, about whom he is less enthusiastic.[43] The latter, he says, are not "likely source[s] of moral entrepreneurship."[44] But Posner, here again, is setting things up so that Rawls and the like are damned no matter what they do. The more unlike Nietzsche and MacKinnon these philosophers are, the more useless. The more like them, the less rational.

Consider the following conundrum: is Posner's own attempt to stigmatize various sorts of advocacy as "nonrational" an example of rational argumentation or of polemical strategy? I have no idea how to answer that question, and see no point in trying to do so. For I would say about criteria of rationality what Posner says about moral principles: they are "just the fancy dress of workaday social norms that vary from society to society."[45]

In the sixteenth century, it was only rational to test astrophysical or biological theories against holy scripture. We can rightly claim to be more rational than Copernicus's contemporaries if that means simply that our beliefs about what to test against what—and, more generally, of what is relevant to what—are true, whereas many of theirs were false. Our social norms are indeed better than their social norms. But there is no discipline called "epistemology" that can show this to be the case. Our judgments of progress and of rationality will remain as parochial as our judgments of everything else. Yet the parochial, historically conditioned character of justification is compatible with the eternal and absolute character of truth.

What is the point of dividing the various tactics we use to persuade our fellow citizens into the rational ones and the others? What difference in practice, one can imagine Dewey asking, is this difference supposed to make? Why hang on to the distinction between the cognitive and the noncognitive that the logical positivists tried to enforce—the distinction that philosophers such as Hilary Putnam and Donald Davidson have done their best to discredit? The question of whether it was rational to let Galilean mechanics undermine Christian faith, or whether this was the result of passionate, irrational, Holbachian, and Voltairean polemic, is not worth raising. Neither is the question about whether the suffragettes achieved victory through the use of reason or by virtue of their remarkable single-mindedness.

Consider Posner's claim that "at its best, moral philosophy, like literature, enriches; it neither proves nor edifies."[46] What follows from this? What does it matter whether we say, with Posner, that "moral philosophers are poets and novelists manqué"[47] or instead say that poets and novelists are amateur moral theorists? We know the sorts of things that moral philosophers, poets, novelists, economists, and lawyers have achieved. We know how they did it. We are in a position to evaluate their contributions to culture and to consider how they might best make further contributions. What purpose is served by separating them into rational sheep and nonrational goats?

Posner seems to think that such separation is essential to doing good sociology. Sociology, he tells us, is the "scholarly niche" that his book on moral and legal theory occupies.[48] He describes himself as employing "Weberian insights concerning professionalization and its alternatives, including charismatic moral entrepreneurship,"[49] and as skeptical about "knowledge claims advanced by certain academic disciplines."[50]

Such skepticism, he says, "is a leitmotif of sociology. . . . [Sociologists] insist that what is 'professed' may mask the pursuit of self-interest."[51]

But adopting a Kuhnian view of scientific progress— replacing epistemology with history and sociology of science— has not encouraged skepticism about knowledge claims advanced by physicists. Nor should it. It was only the invidious contrast between natural science and the rest of culture, the contrast that was at the heart of positivism, that made possible skepticism about moral entrepreneurs. From a Kuhnian perspective, a Weberian sociology of suspicion looks like just one more strategy employed by self-interested professionals hoping to carve out a niche within the academy.

The main reason positivism still seems attractive and pragmatism counterintuitive is the belief that criteria of rationality are more than "just the fancy dress of workaday social norms."[52] That conviction is the legacy of passionate single-minded polemics composed by such intellectual entrepreneurs as René Descartes, John Locke, and Kant. These men tried to make the epithet "irrational" do the work previously done by "un-Christian." Their strategy was to insist, implausibly enough, that relations of relevance between propositions are noncontingent and nonlocal; they taught that an innate faculty called "reason" made such relations evident to any honest mind. We, their heirs, are persuaded that thinking Genesis relevant to biology, or Leviticus to morality, is evidence either of irrationality or of dishonesty.

Dewey and Kuhn tried to persuade us that criteria of relevance, and thus of rationality, are social norms. Such norms have changed, sometimes for the worse and sometimes for the better. They will keep right on changing. But we shall never be able to prove that any given change was a good or a bad one. To do so we would have to find an Archimedean standpoint from which to compare our sentences with the things that make them true or false. The pragmatist denial that there is any such relation as "being made true by" amounts to denying that we shall ever find such a standpoint.

———

I have been arguing in this lecture that Posner's refusal to admit that we have made moral progress is a rhetorical gesture that can have no bearing on practice. For moral progress is not an idea we can possibly get out of our heads. Only the lingering influence of science-worship tempts us to try. The positivists agreed with Plato that to have knowledge was to see things under the aspect of eternity, and they then argued that only natural science could do that. But if we can bring ourselves to give up that Platonic view of knowledge, we might become willing to admit that doubts about moral progress are as phony as doubts about the reality of electrons. Once Plato's attempt to escape from time to eternity is abandoned, we are left with nothing but the hope that we will look good to our future selves, and to future generations. Dewey thought that hope was enough.

4

RETHINKING DEMOCRACY

(1996)

My friend, the Brazilian philosopher Luiz Eduardo Soares, has nicely summarized widespread doubts about the possibility of achieving a global democratic utopia. As Soares puts it, "Agreement on the possibility and desirability of mutual understanding and the building of peace through communication has been shaken by recent dramatic developments: the revival of long-repressed hatreds and hostilities embedded in ethnic, religious and nationalist identities, the growing prestige of postmodern skepticism, and the fragility of universalistic conceptions."[1] I agree with Soares that recent developments give reason for being less optimistic about our ability to build a global democratic utopia. But I do not think that they give reason for rethinking democracy.

We cannot, after all, do without utopian visions. Nobody can take politics seriously who does not hope to make things better for future generations, to create a better world for his or her descendants. Nothing should be allowed to displace an old utopian dream save a new and better utopian dream. Even if it is very hard to imagine utopia coming into existence, that is no excuse for giving up the attempt to create it. What else should we do with our lives? What else could give our lives meaning?

Despite the reasons for pessimism which have arisen in recent decades, nobody has sketched a better utopia than the one which has been familiar since the Enlightenment: a cosmopolitan global society, in which war between nations is as inconceivable as war between Burgundy and Provence, or between California and Florida—a society whose members enjoy the kind of freedom, and the kind of mutual respect, which presently make Americans or Frenchmen citizens of democratic nation-states. Tennyson's dream of "the Parliament of Man, the Federation of the World" was a dream of extending the institutions of representative democracy to the human race.

Events in Bosnia, Rwanda, and Russia help one realize how far we are from the fulfillment of that dream, but they do not differ significantly from similar events in Tennyson's time. Nor have they suggested to anyone a different sort of world-order, an alternative utopia which it would be more reasonable to try to bring into existence. Churchill's much-cited bon mot remains the last word: "democracy is the worst form of government except for all those other forms which have been tried from time to time"—and, one can add, all the others which have so far been imagined.

Only one concrete historical development gives one reason, it seems to me, to wonder whether the utopian dream common to Kant and Tennyson still makes sense: this is the fact that we may have reached a point at which the human population is too large for the planet. The needs of five billion people—shortly to become seven billion—may not be satisfiable without exhausting the oceans of their fish and the continents of their forests, and without producing horrific environmental disasters,

disasters which may be followed by famine on an unprecedented scale.

Let us suppose that the situation is as bad as the most pessimistic students of population and resources have suggested. Would this mean that we needed to rethink democracy? The only argument for doing so I can imagine is that the human race now faces a situation which the masses cannot appreciate; so the wise and informed must set democracy aside, take charge, and impose measures which will avert catastrophe. An example of such an undemocratic measure—a measure which it is hard to imagine being approved by referendum—is, for example, the one-child-per-couple limit imposed on China by its Communist rulers.

I think it would be a good idea for this limit on births to be made universal, and that it would also be a good idea to impose strict limits on the amount of energy a country could consume per capita. I grant that it is unlikely, at the present time, that such limits would be voted by the electorate in, for example, France or the US. But it is not impossible that the electorate of both nations may eventually be convinced of the need for such limits by future events.

So the question of whether democracy needs to be rethought in the light of approaching environmental catastrophe is the question of whether we think that there exist wise and informed leaders to whom it would be safer to entrust our efforts than to the whims of often uninformed and prejudiced voters. I have no confidence whatever that such leaders exist, or ever will exist. I would rather take my chances with uninformed voters than with any alternative decision-makers. The more one tries to imagine alternatives, the better democracy looks.

Let me turn now to the question of what Soares calls "the growing prestige of postmodern skepticism and the fragility of

universalistic conceptions." I would summarize postmodern
skepticism in the following four theses:

1. There is no intrinsic character of reality, no one way
   the world is. No description of the world is closer to
   its nature than any other.
2. There is no correspondence to reality to serve as the
   mark of truth. Rather, we call beliefs true when they
   seem better tools than any as-yet-imagined alternative
   beliefs.
3. Interpretation goes all the way down: there is no contrast
   between a fact and an interpretation except degree of
   consensus: a "fact" is a widely accepted interpretation.
4. There is no objective fact about human beings which
   dictates that our biological species should also be a
   moral community. The project of constructing such
   a community is one interpretation of the significance
   of the human existence among others.

These theses would have been acceptable to Nietzsche, Heidegger, and Foucault, and also to William James and John
Dewey. They are the common ground shared by American
pragmatism and post-Nietzschean European thought. As a
good pragmatist, I embrace all four of them. I am deeply skeptical about the philosophical notions which were in vogue among
the rationalists of the Enlightenment: "Reality as it is itself,"
"Truth as independent of human needs," "Science as the area of
culture which puts us in touch with Reality," and the like.

But this does not make me skeptical about democracy. My
devotion to democracy is not based on philosophical grounds,
but on my suspicion of the various alternatives. Philosophical
skepticism about Enlightenment rationalism is shared by social
democrats like James and Dewey and by philosophers like

Nietzsche and Heidegger, who were sympathetic to fascism. Their philosophical views did not dictate their political views, nor should they have. It is naive to think that adopting rationalist views about such topics as truth, reason, and human nature will act as a bulwark against the forces of darkness. Philosophy and politics are simply not that closely linked.

The reason postmodern, or pragmatist, skepticism may seem to endanger democracy is that the democratic utopia first glimpsed in the eighteenth century has traditionally been described in the rhetoric of Enlightenment rationalism. That rhetoric has gradually superseded religious rhetoric, as notions like "human dignity" and "the demands of reason" took the place of notions like "made in the image of God" and "according to the Will of God," and as respect for science took the place of respect for the Church.

Postmodern or pragmatist philosophy stands to science-centered rationalism as the latter stood to religious thought. It is a further stage in the process of secularization: the process of convincing mankind that human beings must make their own way in the universe, guided by nothing save the results of past experiments, and motivated by nothing save the hope of making human life happier, freer, and more beautiful. From the postmodern or pragmatist point of view, notions like "Reason" and Truth" are substitutes for God—names for a nonhuman authority which is on the side of human freedom. Skepticism about these notions is skepticism about the claim that there is any such authority, and about the idea that we need to picture ourselves as in touch with such an authority in order to have the strength to go on.

Postmodernist skeptics who are also enthusiasts for democracy, as were James and Dewey, view their skepticism about rationalistic philosophy in the way that Voltaire, Diderot, and

Tom Paine viewed their skepticism about the Church: as a way of clearing obstacles out of the way of human progress, a way of helping human beings to stand on their own feet. I view it in the same way. But it is important to realize that philosophical disagreements about the best rhetoric in which to praise democracy should not be allowed to interfere with the project of constructing a global democratic utopia.

Some of those who throw themselves into that project describe themselves as obeying the Will of God; others describe themselves as obeying a Moral Law dictated by the immutable nature of human reason; still others, like myself, describe themselves as hoping to increase the quantity and quality of human happiness.

These three groups have no need to settle the philosophical issues which divide them: either those which divide the Age of Faith from the Age of Reason, or those which divide the Age of Faith from the Age of Postmodern Skepticism. Just as modern democratic societies have learned that religious differences are compatible with political unity, so they should realize that the same goes for philosophical differences.

To return to the quotation from Soares with which I began, I do not think that philosophical universalism—the doctrine that something intrinsic to our membership in the species dictates respect for every other member of the species—is more essential to our hopes for global democracy than the belief that we are all children of the same Heavenly Father. I should like to interpret both philosophical and religious universalism as useful, but optional, ways of expressing such hopes, rather than as assertions upon whose truth those hopes depend.

5

FIRST PROJECTS, THEN PRINCIPLES

(1997)

When I first went into philosophy, I was looking for first principles. I thought that if you could get the right principles, everything else would fall into place. I was wrong. I gradually realized
that it is only when things have already fallen into place that you
can figure out what principles you want. Principles are useful
for summing up projects, abbreviating decisions already taken
and attitudes already assumed. But if you are undecided between alternative projects, you are not going to get much help
from contemplating alternative principles. (Consider, for example, the unexceptionable but conflicting moral principles
cited by each side in the abortion debate.)

Plausible principles are usually too uncontroversial to help
one decide which projects to support. I suspect that anybody
who thinks of him or herself as leftist would be happy with the
most famous principle put forward by a political philosopher
in recent decades, John Rawls's Difference Principle: "Social
and economic inequalities are to be arranged so that they are
both (a) reasonably expected to be to everyone's advantage, and

(b) attached to positions and offices open to all."[1] The trouble is that most people on the right are happy with it too.

You do not encounter many Republicans who tell you that we shall always have the poor with us, that deep inequalities are necessary for the successful functioning of the economy. Rather, Republicans argue (and most of them actually believe) that since the best poverty program is a thriving economy, and since such an economy requires that people who have money send it to their stockbrokers rather than to the government, re-distributionist measures will not be to the advantage of the least advantaged. Such measures, they say, even though adopted with the best of intentions, turn out to violate Rawls's principle.

When we on the left argue with Republicans who take this line, it is not about principles. Rather, we insist that a thriving economy can afford redistributionist measures, and that a rising tide will raise all boats only if the government constantly inter-feres to make sure it does. All the fruitful arguments are about facts and figures, about the concrete consequences of the passage of specific pieces of legislation.

A political left needs agreement on projects much more than it needs to think through its principles. In a constitutional de-mocracy like ours, leftist projects typically take the form of laws that need to be passed: laws that will increase socioeconomic equality. We need a list of First Projects—of laws that will rem-edy gaping inequalities—much more than we need agreement on First Principles.

If most of the leftist magazines and organizations, and most of the labor unions, could agree on a short list of laws that urgently need passage—bills that had been, or were about to be, put before Congress or the state legislatures—maybe the term "American left" would cease to be a joke. If the Americans for Democratic Action, Common Cause, the New Party, the

Democratic Socialists of America, the Gay and Lesbian Alliance Against Defamation, NOW, the NAACP, and all the others could get together behind a short but far-reaching People's Charter, the resulting alliance might be a force to reckon with.

Once upon a time, everybody who thought of themselves as being on the left could tell you what laws were most needed: an antilynching law, an anti–poll tax law, the repeal of the Taft-Hartley Act, Ted Kennedy's national health insurance law, and so on. Nowadays, my leftist students are hard put to name any laws whose passage they think urgent. They do not seem interested in what bills are before Congress or the state legislatures. Their minds are elsewhere: on what they call "cultural politics." It's easy to talk to them about individualist versus communitarian values, or multiculturalism versus monoculturalism, or identity politics versus majoritarian politics, but it is not easy to get them excited about, for example, a proposed law that would remove obstacles the federal government now places in the way of union organizers.

Unless the American left can pull itself together and agree on a concrete political agenda, it is not likely to amount to much. Most leftist journals of opinion, and most leftist professors and students, share the tacit conviction that nothing can be done, that "the system" is hopeless. The idea that the trade union movement might be revived and become the center of leftist politics strikes them as farfetched. The suggestion that the country is still in basically good shape, and still has a fighting chance to break the power of the rich and greedy, seems to them naive.

We need to stop airing these doubts about our country and our culture and to replace them with proposals for legislative change. For our only chance of making either the country or the culture better is to do what our forebears did: keep trying, despite the lethargy and the selfishness, for a classless and caste-less society.

This is what the left did, in fits and starts, from the Progressive Era up through the social legislation that Lyndon Johnson shoved through Congress in the midsixties. It has not succeeded in doing much along these lines in the past thirty years. Unless the left achieves a few successes, it will never recover its morale and will gradually become even more of a joke than it is now.

The only way to achieve such successes is to retrieve the votes of the Reagan Democrats, the bubbas and the high-school graduates and dropouts who resent and despise the colleges and universities as much as they resent and despise the politicians. These people, male and female, black and white, are trying desperately to support households on (if they have enough luck to achieve the national average) $32,000 a year. They need help. They need, for example, unbribed elected officials, health insurance, and better schools for their kids. They know perfectly well that they need these things. The left could make itself useful by offering some detailed advice on how to get them.

Those three needs are good candidates for the first three items on a list of First Projects. The first of them should top that list, since most of the present socioeconomic inequities are held in place by bribes paid by the rich to politicians, bribes that the poor will never be able to match. What is delicately called "campaign finance reform" is the issue on which there is most agreement among all sorts and conditions of Americans: rage at unashamed bribe-taking unites the dropout and the doctor, the plumber and the professor. Most of their cynicism about our system comes from the knowledge that bribery is a way of life inside the Beltway—as taken for granted by the unions and the leftist lobbyists as it is by the Christian Coalition.

Suppose somebody like Paul Wellstone or Barbara Boxer introduced a discarded section of the McCain-Feingold Act— the one stipulating that a candidate cannot appear on TV except during free time provided by the networks, which is mandated in exchange for the broadcasters' license over chunks of the electronic spectrum. Suppose he or she titled it "An Act to Prevent the Bribing of Candidates." Suppose the unions proclaimed that from now on they would pay bribes only to politicians who supported this measure—candidates who would help ensure that unions would no longer need to spend their members' dues on bribes. Suppose the unions promised, once that measure was passed, to spend the money previously used for bribery on getting out the votes of their rank and file in favor of the legislation that would do their membership the most good.

Another obvious candidate for such legislation is universal health insurance—the issue that Bill Clinton rode to victory, played around with, and then forgot about. The poorest fifth of the country still has no medical insurance, and the rest of us are supporting hordes of insurance-company employees—people hired to deny us as much care as they possibly can. Despite retrenchments made in Britain, Scandinavia, and elsewhere, no other industrialized democracy would even contemplate dropping universal health insurance. Visitors from Europe and Canada simply cannot believe what happens when uninsured Americans get sick.

Clinton's failure to get his medical care plan through Congress is being treated like a $300 million movie that flopped ludicrously at the box office, rather than as the national tragedy it was. At this point, the details of a new proposal do not much matter—the old Kennedy single-payer bill might do as well as any. If the left would pick such a bill, drag it into every political conversation, and demand to know the position of every candidate for national office on it, we might finally be able to do what Truman hoped to do: make sure there are no charity cases, that anybody who walks into a hospital has the same rights to the same treatments.

What should be the third item on a list of First Projects? Perhaps it should be the equalization of opportunity in primary and secondary education—something that can only be had if we drop the absurd institution of local financing of schools. If ever an arrangement flew in the face of the Difference Principle, that system of financing does. It ensures that the quality of a child's education is proportional to the price of her parents' home. The courts of New Jersey and Texas have tried to get the suburbs to kick in some money to repair and staff the schools in the urban ghettos and the rural slums, but without much success.

If a kid grows up in a house with some books and a pervading sense of economic security, she already has quite enough of an educational advantage. She does not deserve the additional boost of cleaner, newer, and safer school buildings, or better-paid and less-harassed teachers, than are enjoyed by students in the ghettos. There is no widely disseminated comprehensive plan for equalizing educational opportunity in this country, but we desperately need one.

So much for my suggestions about items that might head the list of First Projects for the US left. Maybe they are the wrong items or are arranged in the wrong order. But at least they share one feature: they are all projects designed to bring the United States up to the level of socioeconomic equality enjoyed by most of the citizens of the other industrialized democracies.

Lots of countries, long ago, adopted laws along the lines of the three I have outlined. In those countries, candidates get radio and TV time for free, during relatively short campaign periods. There are no medical charity cases; medical care is the right of all citizens. To them, the vast disparities between America's suburban and inner-city schools are unimaginable.

These countries have problems, and their citizens are worried. But they have done what we haven't done. They have conceded, grudgingly but steadily, that the best use to make of a thriving economy is to use tax money to increase socioeconomic equality; to make it easier for poor children to get the same life chances as rich children. If the left would unceasingly offer invidious comparisons between Canadian and US health care, between the French *écoles maternelles* and our lack of daycare, between British political campaigns and ours, maybe some headway could be made.

John Dewey hoped that democratic politics would cease to be a matter of batting plausible but contradictory principles back and forth. He hoped that it would become a matter of discussing the results, real or imagined, of lots of different social experiments. The invidious comparisons I am suggesting amount to saying: Look, a lot of good experiments have been run, and some of them have been pretty successful. Let's give them a try. This rhetoric, when combined with a short, easily memorizable list of laws that need to be passed, might give my students a rallying point. It might help some candidates for the Democratic nomination resist the steady shift of the political center toward the right.

That shift toward the right is likely to continue—and the poor will keep right on getting poorer—despite the fact that all our politicians subscribe to all the good old egalitarian principles. New principles will not help reverse this shift, but the success of a few key experiments might.

II

AMERICAN POLITICS

6

DOES BEING AN AMERICAN GIVE ONE A MORAL IDENTITY?

(1998)

When I use the term "moral identity," I have in mind our habit
of using the name of one or another group to which we belong
as a reason for doing or not doing something. This is typically
a group to which we are proud to belong, membership in which
we would not surrender lightly. We often invoke our sense of
solidarity when justifying our actions to others, and sometimes
even to ourselves. For example, a devout friend of mine, who
refuses to give lectures or attend conferences on Sundays, explains himself by saying, "We Calvinists simply do not do that."
When urged to cross a picket-line, a truck-driver might say,
"Nobody from my local would ever do that." When people want
to criticize us for doing something they find repellent, they
often pose not only such rhetorical questions as "How can you
call yourself a decent human being?" but "How can you call yourself a Christian?" or "a liberal," or "a teacher." In an earlier time,
they used to ask, "How can you call yourself a gentleman?"

We all belong to many different groups, and pride in membership in many of them contributes to our sense of who we are, and thus of what sorts of thing it is appropriate for us to do. Since the rise of the nation-state, national citizenship has played a prominent role of this sort. We often say such things as "The news this morning made me ashamed of my country" or "No true-born Briton would even think of doing such a thing" or "That seems un-American" or "That is unworthy of a German." Some people who took pride in being German lost their identification with their nation when they learned about the Holocaust. Back in the sixties, some Americans who had previously taken pride in being Americans found themselves unable to do so after they had reflected on what was happening in Vietnam.

If one lives under a dictatorship, it is a bad thing to let one's citizenship contribute to forming one's moral identity. If one lives in a functioning constitutional democracy, I would argue, it is an unequivocally good thing. It amounts to being idealistic about one's country, something citizens of a democracy ought to be. To abandon such idealism amounts to opting out, to becoming an ironic spectator of the nation rather than a participant in its political life.

About a hundred years ago, William James, briefly carried away by his disgust at our seizing the Philippines from Spain, anticipated the reaction of the sixties radicals to Vietnam. He decided that there was no longer anything special about being an American, and came close to saying that being an American was no longer part of his moral identity. He wrote as follows:

> We used to believe . . . that we were of a different clay from other nations, that there was something deep in the American heart that answered to our happy birth, free from the

hereditary burden which the nations of Europe bear, and which obliges them to grow by preying on their neighbors. Idle dream! pure Fourth of July fancy, scattered in five minutes by the first temptation. In every national soul there lie potentialities of the most barefaced piracy, and our own American soul is no exception to the rule. Angelic impulses and predatory lusts divide our heart exactly as they divide the hearts of other countries.[1]

James said that when we decided to become one more imperialist power, we had "vomited up" the Declaration of Independence and the Farewell Address. "American memories," he concluded, "no longer serve as catchwords." So, he concluded, we American intellectuals must find our moral identities in an international movement rather than in something specifically American. James ended his address as follows:

> The great international and cosmopolitan liberal party, the party of conscience and intelligence the world over, has, in short, absorbed us; and we are only its American section, carrying on the war against the powers of darkness here, playing our part in the long, long campaign for truth and fair dealing which must go on in all countries until the end of time. Let us cheerfully settle into our interminable task.[2]

I suspect that James may well have reflected, in later years, that his rage at what seemed his country's self-betrayal had led him into overstatement. For he was quite wrong when he said that American memories "no longer served as catchwords."

The memory of Lincoln, to take the most obvious example, was still eminently serviceable. Edgar Lee Masters's *Spoon River Anthology*, published in 1914, took up the strain of Whitman's "When Lilacs Last in the Dooryard Bloom'd." Putting his own feelings about Lincoln in the mouth of Anne Rutledge, he ends her epitaph with the lines:

> I am Anne Rutledge that lies beneath these weeds
> Beloved in life of Abraham Lincoln—bound to him
> Not by union, but by separation.
> Bloom forever, O Republic! from the dust of my bosom.[3]

A few years before Masters's *Anthology* appeared, Herbert Croly had said, in *The Promise of American Life*, that Lincoln was the first national politician to proclaim "that American nationality was a living principle rather than a legal bond" and that Lincoln had "cut the ground out from under the traditional point of view of the pioneer, which had been to feel patriotic and national, but to plan and agitate for the fulfillment of local and individual ends."[4]

Croly said that Lincoln "qualified as a national hero" by combining "specific efficiency with supreme kindliness of feeling."[5] He gave Lincoln the credit for the fact that "the higher American patriotism . . . combines loyalty to historical tradition and precedent with the imaginative projection of an ideal national Promise."[6] Croly thought that Promise was in danger of being broken because of "the prodigious concentration of wealth, and of the power exercised by wealth, in the hands of a few men."[7] Croly invoked the memory of Lincoln in order to plan and agitate for social legislation which would redistribute wealth, power, and opportunity. By calling his new magazine the *New Republic*, he tried to call up the power of the same catchword which Masters was to invoke in his poem: "Bloom forever, O Republic! from the dust of my bosom."

James might have reflected that not only were the old catchwords still usable by the "American sector" of the "great international and cosmopolitan liberal party," but that that sector of the party would not be able to conform to its own ideals of democracy unless it used such patriotic catchwords. Political action within a democratic country requires their use. If patriotic idealism goes, so does the possibility of substantial reform through the democratic process. As long as there are nation-states, only national governments will have the power to accomplish the goals set forward by a cosmopolitan and international liberal party. A democratically elected national government will use its power for those ends only if the electorate sees those ends as required by the nation's moral identity. Catchwords which both highlight national memories and summarize national ideals are indispensable for encouraging and shaping such an identity. That is why James was too hasty, and why, seventy years later, the radicals who began to spell "America" with a "k" were too hasty.

Croly tried to persuade his fellow citizens that, as he said, "the American of today and to-morrow must remain true" to the nation's traditional vision. But, he went on to say, we "must be prepared to sacrifice to that traditional vision even the traditional American ways of realizing it."[8] His point was that the traditional way of realizing this vision was to ensure individual freedom by keeping government small, and making it impotent to affect the distribution of wealth. Croly appealed to the communitarian elements in the national tradition against the libertarian elements. He hoped thereby to get the voters to be willing to increase the power of government to solve what he called "the social problem." This was the problem of how to prevent the United States from becoming an oligarchy.

Croly was working the vein described by my University of Virginia colleague, the labor historian Nelson Lichtenstein, when he said, "All of America's great reform movements, from the crusade against slavery to the labor upsurge in the 1930's,

defined themselves as champions of a moral and patriotic nationalism, which they counterposed to the parochial and selfish
elites which stood athwart their vision of a virtuous society."[9]
This vein is still being worked. Nowadays, the present time, the
American sector of the great international and cosmopolitan
liberal party is trying to keep intact the implicit constitutional
changes wrought by Croly's heirs—the ideologues of the New
Deal. This sector is trying to keep the US government big and
strong enough to prevent a new parochial and selfish elite, the
one Michael Lind calls "the overclass," from becoming an entrenched and omnipotent oligarchy.

The American sector is also trying to carry through on the project Woodrow Wilson called "keeping the world safe for democracy." This catchword was ridiculed by those who saw World War
I as a swindle run for the benefit of arms manufacturers, and saw
the Treaty of Versailles as a combination of blunder and sell-out.
But it was revived for use in World War II—a considerably more
plausible war than its predecessor. It still meant a great deal to
those who hoped, in the late 1940s, that the United Nations
could do what the League had not. It was ridiculed once again
in the '60s, when American leftists pointed out that Ho Chi
Minh had used Jeffersonian catchwords in vain when appealing
for American help in gaining independence from the French,
and that the CIA's overthrow of Arbenz merely kept Central
America safe for the United Fruit Company.

Successive waves of ridicule, however, have not produced a
better catchword, a better summary of the aims proper to
American foreign policy, the aims that express the point of
being an American. The idea that America has a mission to
make the world peaceful and democratic lay behind our initiatives in Somalia and Bosnia. Those who hope that the US
will try to turn the UN into a genuine peace-keeping organ-

ization, rather than an occasional front for US policy, still invoke Wilson's ideals.

Nor do we have better catchwords for use in domestic matters than those used by Croly and others in the Progressive Era. We still want a classless society, a society in which all American children have the same chances in life. Writers like Jonathan Kozol are still insisting that the "savage inequalities" between suburban and ghetto schools is a betrayal of what America was supposed to be. There is an unbroken continuity between Jacob Riis's book *How the Other Half Lives* at the end of the last century and Kozol's books at the end of this one, just as there is an unbroken continuity between attempts to get the American government to help the German Jews in the 1930s and attempts to get it to aid the Kurds, the Bosnian Muslims, and the Tutsis in recent years.

Though a lot has happened between Croly's time and the present, the American sector of the international and cosmopolitan party which James described is still working for the same ends, using the same catchwords, and invoking the same historical memories. The most powerful rhetorical tool available to the members of this sector is still the insistence that America stands for a democratic ideal, and that the threats to this ideal are socioeconomic inequality at home and blood-soaked dictators and warlords abroad. The banality of this ideal, and of the rhetoric which describes those threats, should not be allowed to invalidate the catchwords, nor to diminish the memories.

It has become popular among American intellectuals to say that everything is different now, because we are living in a postindustrial age, a multicultural society, a postmodern epoch, and postmodern society, and within a globalized economy that has rendered the nation-state obsolete. But I find it hard to see what difference to our choice of political initiatives any of these purported changes are supposed to make.

The difference between Henry Ford and Bill Gates has little to do with the need to increase socioeconomic equality. The fact that the immigrants who are being employed and promoted over the heads of the African-American descendants of the slaves are Nicaraguan or Vietnamese rather than Irish, Polish, or Italian does nothing to make the elimination of the black-white caste system less urgent. The differences between the philosophical ideas and artistic images of our time and those of the Progressive Era are the merest froth on the surface when compared with the deep similarities between political issues. The governments of the purportedly obsolete nation-states are still the only bodies capable of passing laws and waging war. Laws and wars are still the only means we have to increase equality and freedom and to frustrate oligarchs and tyrants.

It is also popular among American intellectuals to say that we are now in an era in which identity politics, the politics of recognition, has replaced an older sort of politics. But this seems just false. There was as much identity politics at the beginning of the century as now. Feminism, the activities of organizations like the NAACP, the struggle by various ethnic groups to seize control of the political machines in the big cities, and the massacre of one ethnic group by another around the globe, were as much features of the year 1898 as of the present. The struggle of marginalized groups to be recognized by dominant groups was as familiar then as now.

As I see it, it would be well for American intellectuals who hope to contribute to our political life to pay more attention to continuities in our national life than to discontinuities. They should stop being afraid of banality, and stop worrying about whether they are up to date. They should spend more time recuperating national memories and time-honored catchwords, and less time offering sophisticated new diagnoses of our situation.

They should be less afraid of complicity with evil, and more concerned about doing good by whatever means lie to hand.

For example, they should acknowledge that Croly, Wilson, and FDR did a lot of good, even though all three were viciously racist. While regretting that the majority of union members made the stupid mistake of voting for Nixon in 1972, they should acknowledge that the labor unions have done more good for the country than all us academics, and have made far greater sacrifices in doing so. They should acknowledge that there are a lot of straight white working-class males out there who might well become persuaded that it is their moral duty, as good Americans, as loyal citizens of a country with a democratic mission and a generous heart, to vote for gay rights legislation, just as there were a lot of such males who eventually became persuaded to vote for women's suffrage.

It would help the intellectuals do these things if they became less afraid of being unashamedly patriotic. There is no reason for us to deny that our country has been racist, sexist, homophobic, imperialist, and all the rest of it. But there is every reason to remember that it has also been capable of reforming itself, over and over again, and to use such memories as an aid in "cheerfully taking up our interminable task." The historical memories of those successes ought to be enough to make it possible for us to incorporate our American citizenship into our moral identities.

7

DEMONIZING THE ACADEMY

(1995)

Among the many convenient targets that Republican politicians and intellectuals have at their disposal, the one at which they direct their fire with perhaps the most delight is the academy. George Will, William Bennett, and other right-wing thinkers never tire of recounting the follies of professors, and of portraying them as naive, duped, and possibly duplicitous. The right has made especially clever and effective use of the widespread suspicion of multiculturalism. A large portion of the American middle class has been made to believe that the universities are under the control of a "political correctness" police. This false belief has made it easier for the racists, the sexists, and the homophobes to dismiss their opponents as far-out, self-intoxicated radicals—out of touch with the sound common sense of mainstream America.

There is reason to view multiculturalism with alarm—but only mild alarm. The real danger comes from those who are trying to create a monster from what is, at worst, a nuisance. Multiculturalism began to go sour soon after it was invented. It started out as one more attempt to get white middle-class males to behave better toward the people they enjoy shoving around—black and brown people, women, poor people, recent immigrants, homosexuals. It hoped to encourage these groups to take pride in themselves rather than accept the derogatory descriptions that the white males had invented for them. By now, however, it has turned into an attempt to get jobs and grants for psychobabbling busybodies.

The movement began in colleges and universities as an attempt to make room for courses and programs in African-American Studies, Hispanic Studies, Women's Studies, Gay and Lesbian Studies, and the like. This attempt succeeded, and the results have been fruitful. On the campuses, particularly those where such programs exist, there is less humiliation of blacks and browns, less condescension to women, and more safety for homosexuals than anywhere else in society. And these programs are often staffed by some of the liveliest, most interesting, and most devoted teachers.

A debilitating mistake was made, however, when academics began to campaign for compulsory undergraduate courses that would "sensitize students to cultural differences." There is a big difference between offering a tempting smorgasbord of courses designed to help students grasp what the strong have been doing to the weak, and telling them that they must take such courses. It is the difference between gently suggesting, as universities always have, that attitudes acquired at home may need supplementation or correction, and telling undergraduates that they are sick and need treatment. It is one thing to treat students as fellow citizens who might be persuaded to think and act differently than their parents. It is quite another to insinuate that they have been psychologically damaged. Where proposals to make sensitivity training compulsory have gone through, they have boomeranged. The students have quickly come to despise the "compulsory chapel requirement" and to distrust the courses that fulfill it.

In contrast to such facile exercises in "sensitivity," genuine discussion about the divisions in American society would concentrate on disparities of power rather than differences in culture. It would involve stories about how the WASPs have shoved the non-WASPs around, how the men have shoved the women around, how the whites enslaved the blacks, and how the straights beat up the gays. It would emphasize, for example, the fact that property-tax-based public-school financing ensures that the life chances of children in black cities will continue to be vastly inferior to those of children in white suburbs.

Multiculturalism, however, is obsessed not with the suffering but with the "identity" of the groups that have been shoved around. Starting from the admirable idea that black children should learn about Frederick Douglass, Harriet Tubman, and W. E. B. Du Bois, it ends up with the dubious recommendation that a black child should be brought up in a special culture, one peculiar to blacks. Starting from the thought that white children too should know about heroic African-Americans, it ends up with the self-fulfilling prediction that they will remain separated from their black contemporaries not just by money and life chances but by a "difference of culture."

But it is not to the advantage either of our country or of those whom it still treats as second-class citizens to urge, as the multiculturalists do, that we think of the United States as "a salad rather than a melting pot." The simple, straightforward, vicious, terrifying racism that still forces most blacks and browns to struggle desperately, and often hopelessly, for jobs, status, and security is not a result of failure to "recognize cultural diversity." As in the rest of the world, it is a way of ensuring that the descendants of those presently in power will always, automatically, have an advantage because of their easily recognizable, desirable color. Racism, here as elsewhere, increases as soon as jobs and opportunities decrease, and lessens as they increase. If racism ever ends in the United States, it will be as a result of enduring affluence.

In the meantime, it can be mitigated only by appealing, as Martin Luther King Jr. did, to whites' sense of justice toward their fellow Americans. Teaching both black and white children what African-American men and women have done for their country makes such an appeal. Teaching them that the two groups have separate cultural identities does no good at all. Whatever pride such teaching may inspire in black children is offset by the suggestion that their culture is not that of their white schoolmates, that they have no share in the mythic America imagined by the Founders and by Emerson and Whitman, the America partially realized by Lincoln and by King.

That mythic America is a great country, and the insecure and divided actual America is a pretty good one. As racist, sexist, and homophobic as the United States is, it is also a two-hundred-year-old functioning democracy—one that has overcome divisions and mitigated inequalities in the past and may still have the capacity to do so. But by proclaiming the myth a fraud, multiculturalism cuts the ground out from under its own feet, quickly devolving into anti-Americanism, into the idea that "the dominant culture" of America, that of the WASPs, is so inherently oppressive that it would be better for its victims to turn their backs on the country than to claim a share in its history and future.

Although multiculturalism, as a political movement, is guilty of certain blunders and excesses, its critics have greatly exaggerated the threat it poses and the influence it wields. In his recent book *Dictatorship of Virtue*, Richard Bernstein, one of the best reporters at the *New York Times*, writes that "ideological multiculturalism" has brought about "a great inversion in American intellectual life," so that

> whereas before the oppressive force came from the political right, and had to do with a particular view of patriotism, standards and traditional values, the threat of intellectual tyranny now comes from the left, and it now has to do with collective guilt, an overweening moralism and multiculturalism. The danger to such things as free speech and genuine diversity of opinion is no longer due to conservatism; it is due to the triumph of a modish, leftist, moralistic, liberalism.[1]

Nothing in reality (or in Bernstein's book) justifies that last, utterly misleading sentence. Although the book does show that there are more shallow, pated, resentful multiculturalists around than one might have thought, and that they have managed to get control of a primary school system here and a university English department there, the well-organized, well-financed, and very energetic religious right is a hundred times more threatening to free speech and diversity of opinion than all the multiculturalists put together.

Allies of the religious right and conservative intellectuals would like to persuade the public that Allan Bloom was right in suggesting that the universities are under the control of a "Nietzscheanized left,"[2] and that the life of the mind in America survives only in conservative think tanks. There is, to be sure, such a left; though it has managed to achieve a lot of good, it is remarkably shortsighted and sometimes pretty silly. Still, its members total perhaps 10 percent of university teachers of the humanities and social sciences and perhaps 2 percent of all university teachers.

The right has been astonishingly successful in impugning the integrity of the entire system of higher education by pointing to the frivolity and self-righteousness of this 2 percent. The conservatives have some good points, but their exaggerations and lies are shameless. It is quite true that if you are a recent PhD in the humanities or social sciences, your chances of finding a teaching job are very good if you are a black female and pretty bad if you are a white male. But such preferential hiring has, on balance, been a good thing for our universities. Those black females—few of whom were seen on university campuses during the first two hundred years of US history—include some of our leading intellectuals. It is quite true that an undergraduate occasionally finds herself in a course devoted to leftist political indoctrination, but she can always drop that course—and many do. (There are also, needless to say, courses that consist largely of rightist political indoctrination.) It is also true that the 2 percent continue to write in a barely intelligible jargon. But compared with the ravings of the fundamentalist preachers about God's hatred for gays and lesbians, such prattle is merely quaint.

There is, indeed, a battle for America's future going on—but it is not the one Bernstein describes in his book. It is a battle between those who see the widening gap between rich and poor as a disaster for the country, and those who see it as just what the poor deserve. It is a struggle for the mind of an electorate that is largely coextensive with the suburban white middle class—a middle class terrified by the downsizing of American firms caused by the globalization of the labor market, and by the thought that its children may wind up on the wrong side of the gap. Politicians like the new Speaker of the House, Newt Gingrich, and wowsers like Pat Robertson have capitalized, with the utmost cynicism and with complete disregard for the nation's future, on this terror. One of their strategies is to portray the professoriate as a conspiracy of leftist fools and knaves.

It is greatly to the advantage of Gingrich and Robertson to convince the public that the colleges and universities—the places where blacks and gays, women and recent immigrants are treated best—are eccentric, dissolute, corrupt, and perverse. This enables them to dismiss out of hand the warnings of liberal professors—warnings about creating an underclass without hope and of letting the national agenda be dominated by the fears of the suburbs. Such warnings can be brushed aside by treating the academy as having succumbed to a "modish, leftist, moralistic liberalism." We can expect, in the next few years, to see more and more attempts to discredit the colleges and universities, for the right is well aware that the American academy is now (after the breakdown of the labor movement) the last remaining defender of the poor against the rich and of the weak against the strong.

8

AMERICAN UNIVERSITIES AND
THE HOPE FOR SOCIAL JUSTICE

(2001)

American universities serve two quite different functions. On the one hand, they are cogs in an efficient mechanism for training and credentialing the American middle class. The schools of medicine, law, engineering, nursing, and the like keep the economy and the society going by supplying skilled professionals and by carrying out research projects. On the other hand, the universities, and particularly the departments of humanities and social sciences, are staging grounds for leftist political activity. They contain the largest concentration of people concerned with social justice—people who agonize over the vast disparity in life-chances between the rich nations and the poor nations, and between middle-class Americans and poor Americans.

Students and faculties in those departments often think of themselves as the keepers of the nation's conscience. The most liberal candidates for political office typically have their power base in university towns, and can always count on the university's English department for campaign contributions and canvassing.

Leftist professors are notorious for thinking that they know better than the voters what is good for the country. They often look like moralistic prigs, which is why the right has been able to make political capital out of the academic absurdities lumped under the heading of "political correctness."

The gap between this segment of the academy and the vast majority of the American middle class is well described in a recent book by Richard Posner, a federal judge who is perhaps the most admired member of the American legal profession. Posner is respected for his wide learning and for his intellectual acuity both by conservatives and by leftists like myself. He writes as follows:

> The alienation of the intelligentsia is an old story, but a true one, at least so far as the nonscientific departments of the modern American university are concerned. From the perspective of the faculty of these departments, the average voter is ignorant, philistine, provincial, selfish, materialistic, puritanical . . . superficial, insensitive, unimaginative, complacent, chauvinistic, superstitious, uneducable, benighted politically, prone to hysteria, and overweight. . . . The gulf between the middle class and the academic elite is so wide that the members of the latter class, despite their own intense political and moral disagreements, are at one in their hostility to populism.[1]

By "populism" Posner means the sort of political decision-making that leftists sometimes call "participatory democracy." His point is that leftist professors like myself think that the American middle class includes so many death-penalty enthusiasts, gun nuts, rednecked racists, and homophobes that they cannot safely be trusted with political power. Only the retention of power by an educated elite can mitigate the unthinking, resentful sadism of the masses. So we leftists spend half our time claiming that only leftist political measures can bring about true democracy, and the other half regretting that most of the voters are still so ill-educated that they refuse to support such measures.

Despite his somewhat satirical treatment of the bind in which we leftists are caught, Posner agrees that populism is a bad thing. He hopes that we will never have a participatory democracy. He much prefers the sort of struggle between interest groups which goes on in our legislatures, and the deal-cutting half-measures that are the usual upshot of such struggles. He thinks that the slogan "the rule of the people" is a misleading description of how the US is actually governed, and a good thing too. For American democracy is, and should be, rule by an elite. This elite has always been more or less corrupt, and probably always will be. But this sort of rule is, for all its disadvantages, less disastrous than any other form of government that has been tried so far.

We leftists find it hard to disagree with Posner. For we are only in favor of populism when it is on our side—when it is the protest of the weak against the strong. Typically, it is not. An appeal to the feelings of the masses is more often an appeal to resentment and hatred. US Senator Jesse Helms, for example, is a good example of a successful populist politician. Politicians of that sort aim at dividing the poor into warring factions in order to serve the interests of the rich. In the American South, ever since the Civil War, rich whites have pitted poor whites against poor blacks in order to ensure that they will remain in control of state and local governments.

This technique of dividing and conquering is an age-old populist technique, which is still being employed. Before President Lyndon Johnson joined the civil rights movement, it was the basis for the Democratic stranglehold on the former slave states. After Johnson's switch, that strategy played in important role in molding Republican majorities in the South. Jesse Helms first gained his seat in the Senate by conducting a scurrilous, populist campaign against an incumbent Democrat, Frank Graham. Graham had been the liberal president of the University of North Carolina, and he opposed racial discrimination in a period when doing so was still unusual for a Southern politician. Mocking elitist eggheads is an old populist technique, practiced by Hitler as well as by Helms.

Posner is right to emphasize the discontinuity between the members of the literature, philosophy, and history faculties and the rest of the American middle class. There really is such a thing as political correctness, at least in the sense that faculty members in those departments who are dubious about abortion on demand or gay marriage or affirmative action are often reluctant to make their doubts known. One can make oneself very unpopular with the majority of one's colleagues by expressing doubts on these matters. The atmosphere in such departments is very different from that of most middle-class workplaces in the US. The universities have a different ethos than do the hospitals, the corporate offices, the law firms, and the government agencies. There are leftists in all those places, of course, but they do not set the tone. In certain university departments, they do.

A hundred years ago, the literature, history, and philosophy departments were more central to the self-image and the educational function of US universities than they are now. In those days, the members of those departments were less unanimously leftist than they are now, but those we remember most fondly were the ones who championed leftist causes. William James, for example, was a determined opponent both of racial discrimination and of American imperialism. He was infuriated when President McKinley grabbed the Philippines in the aftermath of the Spanish-American War.

James's collaboration with Mark Twain in the campaign against that incursion into Asia resembled the collaboration of eminent professors of philosophy and literature with literary bohemians like Norman Mailer in opposing the war in Vietnam. In protest movements of this sort, the professors, then and now, hang together with the novelists and the poets and the artists. Their coalition has been known, ever since the word was invented at the end of the nineteenth century, as "the intellectuals." (The term "conservative intellectual," which has come into fashion only in the last few decades, still has an oxymoronic ring, especially in the Third World. There, leftist banners call for unity between workers, the peasants, and the intellectuals. Such banners are immediately intelligible, for they refer to a familiar and long-standing alliance.)

James was quite aware of the gap between the intellectuals and the middle class which Posner describes. It was even more sharply marked in his day than now. But he did not see it as a problem, and he was an unabashed elitist in his conception of how social progress or regress occurred. As he saw it, gifted good men and gifted bad men—people like Jefferson and Hitler—see visions. Then they try to gather support for these visions. The advantage of democracy over oligarchy is that in democracies such visionaries have to win the support of a majority of the citizens, and not just of the powerful. Here is James's account of the relation of the universities, and of their graduates, to their fellow citizens:

Mankind does nothing save through initiatives on the part of inventors, great and small, and imitation by the rest of

us. . . . Individuals of genius show the way, and set the patterns
which the common people then adopt and follow. The rivalry
of the patterns is the history of the world. The democratic problem thus is statable in ultra-simple terms: Who are the kind of
men from whom our majorities shall take their cue? . . .

In this very simple way does the value of our educated
class define itself: we more than others should be able to
divine the worthier and better leaders. In our democracy,
where everything else is so shifting, we alumni and alumnae of
the colleges are the only permanent presence that corresponds
to the aristocracy in older countries . . . "Les intellectuels"!
What prouder club-name could there be than this one?[2]

As a result of James and others picking it up, the term "intellectual" was brought over from French into English. Its proper
use has been contested ever since. Populists like Senator Helms
and journalists like Rush Limbaugh have done their best,
throughout the twentieth century, to make the term into a pe-
jorative. There is a strong populist tradition which insists that
a college education—especially the kind which James called
"humanistic"—is likely to make one incapable of understanding the needs of the uneducated, unable to sympathize with
their feelings and grasp their needs.

James took note of this view when he said that the name
"Harvard" suggested, to many people, "little more than a kind
of sterilized conceit and incapacity for being pleased."[3] He
cheerfully admitted that there was some basis for this impres-
sion, and that colleges and universities in general, and Harvard
in particular, did produce a few socially useless prigs. "But," he
went on to say,

every good college makes its students immune against this
malady. . . . It does so by its general tone being too hearty for

the microbe's life. Real culture lives by sympathies and admirations, not by dislikes and disdains—under all misleading wrappings it pounces unerringly upon the human core. If a college, through the inferior human influences that have grown regnant there, fails to catch the robuster tone, its failure is colossal, for its social function stops: democracy gives it a wide berth, turns toward it a deaf ear.[4]

I think that James's contrast between sympathies and disdains, and between admirations and dislikes, helps one think about the present situation of the leftmost members of American university communities, and about their relation to the rest of US society. The universities are at their best, and speak in a robuster tone, when the dominant political emotion on campus is whole-hearted admiration for heroic actions undertaken outside the university. They are at their worst, and speak in much less attractive tones, when they are filled with disdain for the failure of the rest of the middle class to live up to the university's example. In the last thirty years, unfortunately, disdain has predominated over admiration.

The times when the universities are filled with admiration for heroic achievements are also the times at which the university looks best to the public, and performs the greatest public service. At such moments, the claim of the professors to be the keepers of the nation's conscience ceases to sound absurd. The sort of achievements I have in mind are those of the Rev. Dr. Martin Luther King Jr. and the other leaders of the civil rights movement. The universities' admiration for people like Rosa Parks, Medgar Evers, and Julian Bond changed the tone in which professors and students spoke about their country and its future. In 1963, thousands of buses left hundreds of campuses and headed for Washington to hear King's "I Have a Dream" speech. As they went down the highways, these buses were filled with faculty and students singing "We shall overcome." The universities did not initiate the civil rights movement, but they provided support for it in just the way that James had imagined they might.

A similar wave of enthusiasm had gripped the campuses at the turn of the century when news came of Emilio Aguinaldo's struggle against the American invaders of the Philippines, of his heroic fight to permit the Philippine people to govern themselves, rather than submitting to American overlords who hoped to replace Spanish ones. Another such wave occurred a decade later when the professors who were sympathetic to the Progressive Movement urged support for the strikes being organized by heroes like Eugene Debs. Another occurred when professors and students sympathetic to the New Deal supported strikes organized by Walter Reuther, John L. Lewis, and David Dubinsky. Another such moment occurred when the universities stopped serving grapes in the dining halls because Cesar Chavez had asked them to. The same sort of thing happened when Nelson Mandela asked the universities of the world to divest themselves of investments that might benefit the apartheid regime in South Africa. Admiration for heroes and heroines such as these pervaded American campuses. Students returning home from campus, and arguing with their parents, played an important role in changing government policy and American society.

It helps to remember these pages in the history of American universities, and to use that memory to qualify the assertion, shared by Posner and Limbaugh, that the professors are out of touch with their fellow citizens, and are consumed with elitist disdain. It is good to remember the generous enthusiasm in which the universities became caught up in the visions of men like Debs and King—men of the sort James had in mind when he referred to "Individuals of genius [who] show the way, and set the patterns which the common people then adopt and follow." The people whom James called "the intellectuals" may be elitist, and they may even be snobs, but they have been consistently good at what he called "divining the worthier and better leaders." Some of the great disturbers of the peace upon whom our nation now looks back with pride might never have succeeded had it not been for the tub-thumping of the intellectuals.

James's view of elitism as a necessary evil is reflected in his way of dealing with Posnerian doubts about participatory democracy, the sort of doubts that were being voiced in his day by his friend Henry Adams. James paraphrased Adams's fear of redneck populism in the following passage:

> Vulgarity enthroned and institutionalized, elbowing everything superior from the highway, this, they tell us, is our irremediable destiny. . . . When democracy is sovereign . . . sincerity and refinement, stripped of honor, precedence, and favor, will have to vegetate in sufferance in private corners. They will have no general influence. They will be harmless eccentricities.[5]

Nobody, James admitted, can be "absolutely certain that this may not be the career of democracy." But, he went on to say,

> democracy is a kind of religion, and we are bound not to admit its failure. Faiths and utopias are the noblest exercise of human reason, and no one with a spark of reason in him will sit down fatalistically before the croaker's picture. The best of us are filled with a contrary vision of a democracy stumbling through every error till its institutions glow with justice and its customs shine with beauty.[6]

What James wrote a century ago still expresses the fears and hopes of the sort of leftist professors like myself, the sort of professor whom Posner has in mind. We balance their dread of the resentful and ignorant masses with the thought that in the past century appeals to public opinion initiated by an intellectual elite have made a great difference. Such appeals gave women the vote, ended the lynching of black men, and opened the universities to both women and blacks. American institutions at the end of the twentieth century did not glow with justice, but they were considerably less unjust than in the year 1900. The intellectuals think they themselves deserve a bit of the credit for this change, and they are right.

In what I have said so far, I have been emphasizing the apparent tension between the intellectuals' fear of the uneducated masses and the fact that "democracy" is the name of their faith and of their utopia. The tension disappears if one distinguishes between democracy as the name of a utopia in which the strong no longer oppress the weak and democracy as the rule of the people. Democracy in the first sense is pretty well synonymous with social justice. Democracy in the latter sense is pretty much a myth. The confusion between the two is largely the intellectuals' own fault. They have often pretended to believe in something they do not really believe in at all—the deep wisdom of the people, the sound common sense of the voters. Often they have pretended this even to themselves.

The reason for this pretense is obvious. It is that the most effective way to argue for the superiority of representative democracy over other forms of government is to claim that the masses will vote their interests, and will elect candidates who will improve their lot. The common sense even of the ignorant and badly educated will, so this argument goes, be enough to make them vote for candidates who help them to be better off.

This claim is largely false. It is because the intellectuals have tacitly recognized its falsity that they have always feared populism. But they have been unwilling to simply abandon the claim, since their own hopes for social justice depend on their ability to influence the masses' opinions. On the one hand, leftist intellectuals know perfectly well that the masses are suckers for demagogues like Jesse Helms. On the other hand, the only way they themselves can help bring about institutional change is to tell the masses that certain premises they have always accepted dictate such change—for example, that the doctrine of universal human brotherhood dictates the end of racial discrimination. So they find themselves trying to have it both ways—saying that although at the moment the masses are stabbing themselves in the back, in the long run they will have enough sense to stop doing so.

This double-mindedness seems to me necessary and desirable. It is an expression of the state of mind James described when he said that "democracy is a kind of religion, and we are bound not to admit its failure." Conventionally religious people have to have enough double-mindedness to believe both that there is terrible evil in the world and that that same world is the work of a benevolent and omnipotent creator. They believe both that bad things constantly happen to good people and that God's providence means that everything happens for the best. Such double-mindedness is not a sign of irrationality, but is rather a reasonable compromise between fear and hope.

The people whom James called "the intellectuals" are making the same sort of compromise. For the will of the people is no less puzzling a notion than is the will of God. The religion of divine providence hopes that God will somehow make everything right. The religion of democracy hopes that the people will someday come to their senses. In the meantime, both can only say that their respective object of worship works in mysterious ways.

So far I have been offering a rather general and abstract account of the self-image of leftist American professors and of their role in our nation's cultural and political history. In the space that remains, I want to be more concrete, and to take up three leftist initiatives which have, in recent years, found support in American universities: (1) the attempts to encourage multiculturalism in the curriculum and in the configuration of academic departments in the humanities and social sciences; (2) the protests against the World Trade Organization and the International Monetary Fund that rocked Seattle and, more recently, Genoa, and in which many American students participated; (3) the "justice for janitors" campaign that has sponsored rallies and demonstrations on many campuses. I shall argue that the third of these initiatives is likely to be the most fruitful, because it is the one in which the appeal to public opinion is most likely to be successful.

————

Multiculturalism is a word less frequently heard on American campuses than ten years ago, but the topic still comes up in meetings of faculty senates and of academic departments. However, it was never very clear what this word meant. One reason for this is that it was never very clear what those who said that "every culture is worthy of respect" had in mind. Nobody wanted to claim that Nazi culture, or that of Islamic fundamentalism as practiced by the Taliban, or the culture of the marauding Mongols or Aztecs or Zulus, should be respected. For to have called for such respect would have undermined the criticisms that those who repeated this slogan were simultaneously making of American sexism, racism, and imperialism.

That misleading slogan was really a way of saying, "We need to realize that the culture of the educated classes of Europe, the culture which until recently formed the substance of humanistic education in US universities—the Eurocentric culture that revolved around the lives of wealthy, leisured, white, heterosexual males—is not the only culture with a claim on our attention." But when put in this mitigated form, the slogan was both uncontroversial and pointless. It provided no guidance. For nobody was prepared to argue that every culture worthy of our attention should be incorporated into the undergraduate curriculum, or even that every such culture should be a subject of attention somewhere in every university. There are simply too many such cultures. There is no way in which a single student or professor could become acquainted with more than a tiny fraction of them. Some selection is necessary.

That selection was provided by the political needs of various oppressed groups in the United States. When historians of American higher education look back on the multiculturalist rhetoric that was frequent in American universities in the 1980s and 1990s, they will see it as an awkward attempt to provide a rationale for the emergence during those decades of programs in Afro-American Studies, Hispanic-American Studies, Asian-American Studies, Women's Studies, and Gay and Lesbian Studies. The attempt was awkward because the only rationale that was needed was that various groups which had been given a raw deal by American society could use academic programs such as these in order to help themselves get a better deal. By directing attention to the history of these groups, and to their literary and artistic productions, such programs gradually helped alter the relations between these groups and the rest of American society.

The emergence of these programs was a very good thing both for American universities and for the nation as a whole, but the notion of "culture" was largely irrelevant to their nature and function. That function was political. These programs, as Judith Butler has said, kept the left alive during the Reagan and Bush years. Their existence has produced a whole generation of white male heterosexual college graduates—the part of America that still retains most of the economic and political clout—whose notions about and attitudes toward blacks, women, Hispanics, and gays are appreciably different from those typical of their parents. Such academic programs helped make the US a more decent place. They constitute one of the great contributions of the American universities to American political life.

But there were unfortunate side-effects of the rise of these programs. One was that the attention of leftists was diverted from economic inequality to cultural insensitivity. Leftist professors began to brandish phrases like "the deeply cultural character of the revolution of our times" and to say things like "cultural politics is central to all politics." Leftist political theorists began writing books and articles proclaiming that cultural recognition was one of the principal goals of leftist politics. Because they were themselves, for the most part, specialists in culture rather than economics, they easily persuaded themselves that reciprocal appreciation by Americans of the cultural backgrounds of their fellow-citizens was as important as ensuring that all American have equal educational and economic opportunities. They came to believe that respect for someone's cultural background was as urgent a goal as paying him or her a living wage.

I would argue that cultural recognition is of political importance only when it contributes to rectification of socioeconomic inequality, and that that contribution is marginal. Cultural recognition is not an end in itself, and should not become a goal of leftist politics. In support of this claim, I would cite the similarity between what is likely to happen to the descendants of immigrants from Asia and Latin America with what happened in the course of the twentieth century to descendants of immigrants from Europe.

My hunch is that the children of recently arrived Asian-Americans and Hispanic-Americans are going to intermarry with the descendants of earlier waves of immigration, just as the Poles, the Italians, the Jews, and the Irish immigrants did. As Michael Lind has pointed out, these people will all simply be dubbed "white," and nobody will understand why it was once predicted that in 2050 the majority of Americans would be non-white. Intermarriage is the standard way in which cultural differences become political irrelevant, and is the basis for the claim that America was already, long before the advent of multiculturalism, a pluralist society.

By 2050, millions of middle-class Americans with Vietnamese or Salvadorean grandmothers will be journeying to those countries with the same curiosity as moved me when I traveled to Ireland to look up my grandfather's baptismal record. There will be as much respect for the cultures of those countries as the American descendants of white Anglo-Saxon Protestants have for the culture of Italy.

But, as Michael Lind has also predicted, it seems likely that this process of cultural assimilation will do nothing whatever for African-Americans. They will form the only group that does not get reclassified as "white," and with whom those who are classified as "white" will remain reluctant to intermarry. The incredibly cruel caste system which was created by African slavery is quite likely to survive the creation, as a sequel to the civil rights movement, of a sizable African-American middle class. As long as employers would rather hire a day laborer who has just arrived from Mexico, and whose English is feeble, than one whose African ancestors were brought here in chains three hundred years ago and whose English is perfect, that system will persist. That familiar hiring pattern is, as William Julius Wilson has pointed out, still in place.

Programs in African-American Studies are very unlikely to do anything much to alter it, or to change the laws that make possession of crack a far more serious crime than possession of cocaine, or the laws that permit the armaments industry to unload millions of Saturday night specials onto young, unemployed, despairing black men. If these laws are ever changed, and if black children in the cities ever get to attend safe and clean schools, it will not be because the college-educated whites have become better able to appreciate black history, black literature, and black contributions to American culture. It will be because they have become willing to pay more taxes, and to have those taxes used to promote redistribution of wealth, income, and opportunity across caste boundaries.

———

Such redistribution is the traditional goal of leftist politics, and is the principal means of bringing about social justice. I want to turn now to an initiative that, unlike multiculturalism, is aimed directly at such redistribution. My second example of a leftist strategy that originated on the campuses is the protests against the new world economic order that were made in Seattle, Washington, and Genoa. This is part of the same revulsion at the thought of the rich nations profiting at the expense of the poor ones that motivates the campus boycotts of sneakers and T-shirts that come from Third World sweatshops.

These protests stem, in part, from the realization that national governments have less and less power to control the life-chances of their citizens. For those life-chances are at the mercy of economic developments about which such governments can do increasingly little. Globalization, and the extraordinary fluidity of investment capital, make it impossible for governments to predict or control the course of their own economies. Even rich nations like the US can be thrown into recession, and perhaps into depression, by events which are pretty much out of their control—events such as the collapse of a currency on the other side of the world. Nobody knows what would happen in the US and Europe, for example, if the Japanese yen should collapse in the way in which the Thai bhat and the Mexican peso did. That collapse would be on a scale that would make it impossible for the US Treasury to intervene effectively.

Poor nations, of course, are far more easily endangered. They live in constant fear of decisions by international investors to move production to some country in which wages are even lower and the government even more corrupt. If the workers in Malaysia, for example, demand the equivalent of a dollar an hour, it is easy to build a factory in Laos where they will happily settle for twenty-five cents an hour. The effect is to drain off the entire surplus value of the work done in the Third World into the hands of corporations whose managers and shareholders have no stake whatever in the lives of the people who work in their factories.

There is, obviously, a lot to protest in this situation. Nobody is able to deny that the IMF and the World Bank are assuming that what is good for the multinationals is good for peoples of the world. The assumption is linked to the one which is at the heart of conservative thinking of the sort that lay behind the policies of Reagan and Thatcher—the assumption that the only danger to the freedom and the welfare of the individual comes from the power of the state, and that the market will eventually produce prosperity for all. Both assumptions are, we leftists think, false. Acting on them is a recipe for the continuation, and indeed for the increase, of social injustice.

The problem with the Seattle protests and the Nike boycotts, however, is that they are being made by people who have no alternative policies to advocate, no concrete suggestions about what is to be done. They resemble in this respect the Campaign for Nuclear Disarmament, a movement that produced similar enthusiasm among leftists and then gradually disappeared. The trouble with the Campaign was that nobody could suggest a way of dealing with the possession of a nuclear arsenal by an evil and unpredictable empire such as the USSR except the seemingly crazy policy of mutually assured destruction that the West had adopted. The trouble with the Seattle protests is that nobody has much of an idea what a good global economic setup would be, and by what agencies it might be brought into being.

It is one thing to say, rightly in my opinion, that jungle capitalism on a global scale is likely to be fatal to the life-chances of most of the peoples of the world. It is another thing to propose a different world economic order, one which does not depend upon jungle capitalism as the agency of economic development. Maybe there is such a proposal on the table, but I have not seen it, and I doubt that most of the Seattle protesters could formulate it. But in the absence of such a proposal the Seattle protests cannot become a viable political movement, as opposed to an entirely justified expression of dread. The Campaign for Nuclear Disarmament was a similarly justified expression of dread, but it never became a political movement because nobody could take the idea of unilateral disarmament seriously. Protests like those in Seattle are likely to fizzle because nobody, even ardent leftists, can take seriously the idea of protecting the forests and the seas at the cost of denying a better life to people who are now living on a dollar a day—people who want nothing more than for a sweatshop to open in their home town.

These are the reasons why I do not see much promise in the second of the leftist initiatives I have mentioned. Unlike multiculturalism, the protests against the new economic order are aimed at what seems to me the right target—namely, social injustice. Nothing is a more appropriate object of leftist concern than the monstrously unjust arrangements that drain off most of the surplus labor of people outside of Europe and America in order to permit the Europeans and the Americans to fill their houses with consumer goods. But leftist protests against injustice only get off the ground if they are incorporated in a program for change—a description of an alternative set of concrete arrangements, and a road map showing how we might get there from where we are now.

It is a bad sign that some of the young American leftists who demonstrated in Seattle are reverting to a neo-Marxist rhetoric which calls for "the overthrow of global capitalism." There is no point in asking people to overthrow capitalism unless you can explain what is to be put in its place, and can explain why the alternative is preferable. That is just what the old-timey Marxist revolutionaries were never able to do. Unless and until the critics of globalization come up with either substitutes for the IMF and the World Bank, or else spell out what they would do if they were in charge of those organizations, it is unlikely that the Seattle demonstrations will jump-start a movement in the way that King's Selma march did. We knew, at the time of Selma, just what changes in which laws would remedy the wrongs which the marchers were protesting. We do not know anything like this in the case of the globalization of the economy.

———

Consider, by way of contrast, the campaign for justice for janitors. Campus protests against the university's treatment of its

nonacademic, blue-collar staff have mounted in recent years, as
have attempts to get municipal governments to pay, and require
that their suppliers pay, a living wage. Here the wrong being
done is uncontroversial (badly distributed money) and the
remedy is obvious (fairer shares). Universities have taken, in
recent decades, to contracting out the task of serving food,
cleaning toilets, and the like to organizations that pay the lowest
possible wages and typically provide no benefits at all. This has
weakened what used to be a sense of pride in working for the
university, and a sense of community among its employees. It
has also weakened the ability of nonacademic employees to get
better treatment by becoming members of labor unions.

The students who take part in these protests typically come
from middle-class families. Two-thirds of the freshmen who
matriculated in the fall of last year came from families whose
annual income was above $50,000 per year. Twenty-five percent
called themselves "liberal" and only 18 percent called themselves "conservative," with 50 percent answering "middle of the
road." But 52 percent of those freshman said that they thought that
"wealthy people should pay a larger share of taxes than they do
now." The sense that the people in the dead-end jobs at the bottom
of the academic ladder are being treated unfairly, and that the rich
are having it all their own way, is quite widespread.

Suppose that these protests were taken up by the faculty and
students in university after university. Suppose that the faculty
voted that there should be no raises in faculty pay until the
lowest-paid workers at the university were getting a living
wage—something more like ten dollars an hour than like six—
and until all university workers had the same medical and dis-
ability benefits as the professors got. Suppose the students
voted that they would not protest tuition increases that were
specifically, and demonstrably, used to achieve that level of

wages and benefits. Suppose that both groups joined in demanding that the university stop interfering with attempts by its workers to unionize.

This is easier to imagine happening at the richest universities, the ones with the richest students and the best-paid professors—places like Princeton, Stanford, and Rice. But these rich private universities have often served as standard-setting models for the public universities, and might again. If the "justice for janitors" movement spread beyond this charmed circle, and if it became a matter of pride for a university to be on the list of those who met a set of national standards for decent treatment of workers, it is not impossible that the universities could set a model for the larger society.

All this may be a pipe dream, but the idea of collective bargaining seemed a pipe dream a hundred years ago, and that of desegregation seemed a pipe dream fifty years ago. Sooner or later, after all, the country has to make some attempt to narrow the gap between rich and poor that has been widening in the US for three decades. Widespread public support of the labor union movement helped narrow that gap between 1940 and 1970, but that support has sharply diminished. Some other institutions have to take the lead if it is to be narrowed, since neither Democratic nor Republican administrations have the courage to propose any measures that will do so. The universities are as good a place to start as any.

Let me close by coming back to my earlier remarks about elitism and populism. I said that I agreed with William James's elitist view that the educated, what James called "the college-bred," are better at divining the worthier and better leaders. There is, at the moment, no single charismatic leader such as Cesar Chavez or Martin Luther King Jr. behind whom we leftists can close ranks. But the students who are organizing "justice

for janitors" campaigns in their universities will do until somebody more charismatic comes along. These students are among
the few Americans who retain the vision of an America in which
our institutions glow with justice and our customs shine with
beauty. They are among the few whose faith in the religion of
democracy seems to be still alive. They are well suited to the
role of keeper of the nation's conscience.

9

THE INTELLECTUALS AND THE POOR

(2001)

In this essay I shall make some distinctions between types of contemporary American intellectuals. I divide them into the liberals, the radicals, libertarian conservatives, and cultural conservatives. I shall use the terms "left" and "leftist" to cover both the radicals and the liberals.

American liberal intellectuals have traditionally painted a picture of America as gradually, gloriously improving both its institutions and its customs—making them more just and more beautiful as the decades have gone by. They have then added that these institutions and customs are still much more unjust and ugly than is generally thought, and they have offered suggestions for change. American radical intellectuals have said that the sort of changes we have made in the past—even such vast, quasi-constitutional changes as those produced by the Civil War and by the Great Depression—are insufficient. Radicals are prone to speak of "the system" as something that is going to have to be replaced, rather than speaking of the country as one that we must continue to reform.

By libertarian conservatives I mean people who follow Hayek and von Mises in thinking that the basic political choice is between giving power to the market and giving power to the state, and who see the market as preferable, because less likely to bring about a loss of individual liberty. By cultural conservatives I mean people who are inclined to think that belief in God is essential to morality, and are sure that tolerance for such things as abortion on demand and uncloseted homosexuality are a sign of moral degeneration. These two kinds of conservatives are now, for strategic reasons, allied—though their principles do not dictate any such alliance. There are plenty of libertarian conservatives who favor legal recognition of gay marriages, and (even though no example comes to mind) there seems no reason why there might not be a cultural conservative who accepted the need to enlarge the scope of the welfare state.

To make the distinction I want to draw a little more concrete, consider the question of whether there is any common principle from which one can infer both that the welfare state should be repealed and that homosexual behavior should be considered perverse and wrong. I cannot think of any, yet it is certainly the case that both views are held by most intellectuals who call themselves "conservative" and that the contradictory view is held by most intellectuals who call themselves "liberal." Most of the conservatives would agree with Colin Powell that there is no analogy between keeping blacks out of the military and keeping gays out, whereas most of the liberals would insist that the cases are perfectly analogous. Most of the former would agree that it is more important to eliminate big government than to ensure the right of poor children to be supported by the taxpayers, and most of the latter would disagree. Yet it is not clear what binds these two issues together, except the fact that many people who are well off both hope to pay less in taxes and pride themselves on repressing any homosexual impulses they may have.

Liberal intellectuals typically see an unwillingness to be taxed more heavily as selfishness, and the view that homosexual impulses should always be repressed as sadism. On the traditional liberal view, selfishness and sadism are the two enemies of just institutions and beautiful customs. Whereas the libertarian conservatives see the principal task of the intellectual in politics as adjudicating the relative claims of order and of liberty, and the cultural conservatives see it as reminding us all of the need for unchallengeable moral, religiously grounded, truths, liberals see that task as getting the strong to care about the needs of the weak.

Liberals want to substitute a civic religion, the joyful celebration of a common heritage, common citizenship, and common dreams for the future, for traditional attempts to be on the side of God. When cultural conservatives quote scriptural prohibitions and warnings, liberals always respond with First Corinthians, chapter 13: "charity suffereth long, and is kind." For liberal intellectuals, the point of Christianity was not to save us from sin, but to pave the way for John Stuart Mill's utilitarian morality, and thus for his claim, in *On Liberty*, that any behavior which harms no one but oneself must be left unregulated.

On top of the fourfold distinction I have just made between kinds of intellectuals, I want to place a twofold distinction which cuts across these four kinds. This is the distinction between political intellectuals and philosophical intellectuals. Political intellectuals, in the sense I shall give to this term, are people who take sides on concrete questions which are to be decided by organs of government. Philosophical intellectuals are those who usually do not descend to this level of concreteness, and confine themselves to more abstract reflections on the nature of the state, of power, of Otherness, of virtue, of morality, of history, and the like. This is a crude distinction, but it permits me to frame three crude generalizations.

(1) In twentieth-century America, we have had, and still have quite a few conservative philosophical intellectuals, but very few conservative political intellectuals. We have had a lot of highly educated and articulate conservative cultural warriors, of the caliber of Henry Adams, T. S. Eliot, and Irving Babbitt. But when it comes down to explaining why we should not have a redistributive fiscal policy, or the union shop, or have national health insurance, or desegregation, or gays in the military, these people have tended, and still tend, to pass the buck to the demagogues—the Newt Gingriches and the Rush Limbaughs of their day. Even though some contemporary conservative intellectuals like William Kristol are good at discussing Plato and Aristotle and also good at writing memoranda to Gingrich about how to prevent passage of a national health insurance, they rarely try to connect these two skills. They do not discuss what can be done to alleviate the crowding in hospital emergency rooms, but instead quickly infer from the desirability of getting rid of the omnipotent state to the desirability of defeating all proposals to give the state more power to help the poor. As intellectuals rather than flacks, thinkers rather than manipulators, they prefer to stay at the philosophical level.

(2) Between the Progressive Era and the mid-1960s, America had a lot of liberal intellectuals who were able to move back and forth easily between the political and the philosophical. William James and John Dewey are the most obvious examples, but one could equally well cite Herbert Croly and Woodrow Wilson in the first part of this period, or John Kenneth Galbraith, Arthur Schlesinger, and Sidney Hook at its close. All these people were able to discuss issues of political and moral principle, and

alternative narratives of the great sweep of human history, and to connect this activity with that of arguing for concrete political proposals by reference to the expected consequences of their adoption. They were able to do what their conservative opponents—the Henry Adamses, the Irving Babbitts—did not do: weave talk of principle together with proposals for increasing human happiness. The best these opponents could do was to rebuke the liberals for utopianism and optimism, a rebuke which fell flat in a country which has always dreamed of a utopian future.

(3) Since the rise of the New Left in the 1960s, and the shock of Nixon's defeat of McGovern in 1972, the torch has somehow passed from the liberals to the radicals, and from the political intellectual to the philosophical one. The shock of McGovern's defeat caused many people who went to college in the sixties to decide that American democracy—"bourgeois democracy" as they liked to call it—was hopeless. They decided that the American dream was a consumerist illusion, and that what Croly called "the promise of American life" had been a fraud. They began to view the country of which they were citizens with suspicion rather than love. They have been fighting culture wars rather than arguing for legislation. They have become increasingly priggish, and have begun to confine themselves to academic politics as opposed to real politics, to discussing Difference and Otherness rather than poverty and health care.

———

So much for my three crude generalizations. I can point to their moral by saying that nowadays there is a striking, and regrettable, similarity between right-wing and left-wing intellectuals in the contemporary United States: both of them spend a lot more time on cultural issues than on economic ones. The political right spends a lot of time talking about family values. The political left spends a lot of time talking about cultural diversity. Neither side has anything very concrete to say about how to reverse the growing gap between the rich and the poor, nor about how to keep the country from entering a Weimar-like situation, in which the downsized and disappointed rebel against what has rightly been called a "winner-take-all" system.

The right has little to say because it is financed by the rich, who do not want to be taxed, or otherwise disturbed. Nor do the rich want to be troubled by the thought that they are profiting at the expense of most of their fellow citizens. The rich profit when production of consumer goods is increased; so, as Galbraith pointed out forty years ago, they think that if the economy is in good shape, America must automatically be in good shape. If it takes downsizing of middle managers and exportation of unskilled jobs to keep the American economy efficient, so be it. The rich have no patience with the Galbraith's suggestion that we need to alter the balance between private and public investment.

In the aftermath of the 1960s, leftists began to lose themselves in dreams of "a radically new socioeconomic system." Once it became clear that socialism was a dead letter, and that a capitalist welfare state was the best we could hope for, radicals lost interest in economics. They stopped thinking about what laws should be passed, and began thinking about what they called "issues of race, class, and gender." In practice, this has meant ten thoughts about race and gender for every thought of class. For discussing class means discussing economics, statistics, and policy, and the present academic left, which is more radical than liberal, prefers to discuss philosophy.

While the left and the right bicker over lifestyles, the United States is being divided into what Michael Lind calls "the overclass"—the comfortably off upper 20 percent—and the increasingly desperate bottom four-fifths. The savage inequalities which Jonathan Kozol has described between suburban and urban schools become more savage every year. Modest, commonsensical, economically efficient proposals to help poor people die in congressional committee: for example, Senator Bill Bradley's bill to establish shelters in which pregnant poor women can have fifteen months' worth of care for themselves and their babies. The number of outraged, desperate, vengeful, unemployed ex-middle managers grows to Weimar-like proportions. The effects of the globalization of the labor and capital markets continue to spread, so that more and more jobs which once were assumed to be the property of us Americans are being exported overseas.

Those on the right—the rich and powerful, the people who can afford to bribe legislators to get the laws changed in their favor—have every reason to keep public attention focused on the so-called culture wars. The more they can keep the public talking about values, the less likely it is that there will be time, or newsprint, left over to discuss money. The more you can keep political disagreement focused on whether to let gays serve in the military, or whether to abandon affirmative action, or whether to allow second trimester abortions, or whether to make multicultural curricula compulsory, the less attention will be spent on the distribution of income and wealth. If the right can keep us talking about the terrible effects of postmodern philosophy on young minds, we shall have that much less time to talk about the fact that two people working at the minimum wage will never save enough to buy a house. If conservatives can

convince people that our troubles are due to individual irresponsibility on the part of the poor, nobody may notice that we
have no defense against the social irresponsibility of corporations except government regulation.

For all these reasons, the preference of the right for cultural
over economic issues is unsurprising. What is more surprising
is that the left should let itself be so distracted from its longtime
concern with economic redistribution. But this odd phenomenon is explicable when one remembers that the only truly
stunning victory which the American left has achieved since
World War II has been the achievement of a limited amount of
social equality between blacks and whites, and the creation of
a sizable black middle class. That victory had the unintended
consequence of refocusing the left's attention. Attempts to meet
the needs of women, of gays and lesbians, of Hispanic-Americans,
and of recent immigrants, employed the same rhetoric, and the
same tactics, as had been used by the civil rights movement of the
1950s and 1960s. These were groups whose social and economic
situation was dependent on noneconomic factors.

The success of the left's struggles on behalf of these groups
has been, if not comparable to the success of the civil rights
movement, very considerable. When one considers sexual harassment of women by men, or the ability of gay men and women
to come out of the closet and keep their jobs, it is clear that
things have changed enormously in the last twenty-five years.
On the other hand, much of these changes have been largely
confined to the upper reaches of the middle class. It is a lot easier
for a female lawyer to avoid harassment than for a female policeman, and a lot easier for a gay man to keep a job as a professor
than as a fireman. The universities and colleges have been the
centers of struggles on behalf of minorities and women, and the

results of these struggles have done more for college graduates than for people who did not finish high school.

Even with these reservations, the changes in the treatment of ethnic groups, women, and gays have made our country a morally much better place. But all these changes are in danger as a result of the increasingly desperate economic situation. They are changes which, like the elimination of legally sanctioned racial segregation, were made in an era of relative prosperity, and thus of good feeling. As the benefits of economic growth are shifted more and more toward the top of the income scale, however, there will be less and less good feeling. There will be, instead, more and more receptivity to Rush Limbaugh's rhetoric. People like Limbaugh will persuade more and more white males who cannot find a foothold in the middle class that the improvements in the situation of college-educated women, blacks, and gays have been made at their expense.

10

CAN AMERICAN EGALITARIANISM
SURVIVE A GLOBALIZED ECONOMY?

(1998)

Most of the infrequent contacts between CEOs and philosophy
professors take place on airplanes. These contacts take the form
of exchanges of life-stories between seatmates, exchanges which
mitigate the boredom of flight. Such exchanges provide one of
the few ways in which inhabitants of the academy get a sense of
what the other is doing.

Professors who work in fast-breaking fields like molecular
biology or neopragmatist philosophy are always flying off
to conferences in places like Sao Paolo, Taipei, or Vienna. Our
transoceanic flights are usually in economy class, but we nevertheless have our reward. When we return home we find that the
airlines have sent us upgrade certificates for domestic air travel.
This means that we can sometimes go first class to conferences
in places like Los Angeles or Seattle. We thus get to sit next to
richer and more important people.

My most memorable airplane conversation took place last
year over free drinks in the front cabin of a plane from Charlotte

to Houston. It was with a man who was in the business of exporting American jobs. He was a man of great sophistication and very wide experience—a self-made entrepreneur, who had worked his way up from a working-class background to founder and CEO of a substantial manufacturing company. Having sold the company at a good price to a conglomerate, and not being ready for retirement, he had become a consultant. He now spends his time helping companies relocate their manufacturing facilities in far-away places—mostly in Asia, but sometimes in Europe. Currently he was working on transplanting a factory from a small town in North Carolina to a small town in Slovenia.

My reaction to his story was a mixture of admiration for his obvious ability and enterprise, and incredulity that he would so insouciantly confess to what he was doing. I suggested to him that it might be dangerous to create an economy in which Americans who were not good at being what Robert Reich calls "symbol analysts" could no longer find work, except for minimum wage burger-flipping jobs. I asked him whether the communities which were deprived of their traditional sources of employment had much hope of ever replacing them.

His reply was that American workers were going to have to tighten their belts, since they were no longer competitive on the world labor market. Repeating the usual arguments for free trade, he went on to explain, echoing Marx, that labor was a commodity like any other. It could not be exempted from the global market without producing distortions of the world economy which, in the long run, would work against American interests. It was understandable, he admitted, that American workers should be unwilling to accept wage cuts, but they would find that they had no choice in the matter.

By this time the flight was almost over, and we could not pursue the issues further. But ever since, I have been reading

articles about the globalization of the labor market with fear
and trembling. The last such article was by Edward Luttwak and
was called "Why Fascism is the Wave of the Future."[1] Luttwak's
argument was that the social disruptions which have always
been a product of the operation of free markets were about to
become far more intense than at any period since the early nineteenth century. There is, Luttwak claimed, nothing which the
workers in the industrialized democracies can do for $10 or
DM20 of FF60 an hour which cannot be done just as well for
$1 an hour in Southern China or in Thailand. Those who once
earned those high wages, he predicted, would not tolerate governments that permitted a catastrophic fall in employment and
in the standard of living. They would imitate the behavior of the
Germans at the end of the Weimar period. They would turn to
populist rabble-rousers who would make empty promises, or
else attempt to reinvigorate the economy by starting a war.

Having recently visited Guangzhou, I am pretty sure that
Luttwak was right about the economic facts. I suspect that he
is also right about the sociopolitical consequences of these economic changes. Democracies are at their moral best in periods
when everybody is pretty confident about their own and their
children's future. America's greatest moral achievement of this
century, the end of racial segregation, was possible only because,
in the 1950s and 1960s, the white middle class of the United
States thought that there was going to be enough for everybody, even the blacks. A civil rights movement was not in the
cards during the Depression, the period in which Sinclair
Lewis wrote *It Can't Happen Here*, a marvelously plausible scenario for the coming of fascism in America. That novel is a bit
out of date, but it would not be hard to revise it to provide a
scenario for the United States in the first decade of the twenty-
first century—a decade in which the steady decrease in the

standard of living of the middle class may result in cataclysmic political change.

The gap between the rich and the poor has been widening in the US for twenty years, and by now we live in a time in which 57 percent of Americans think that life will be worse for their children than for themselves. But this is still a vague, dark suspicion. If the globalization of the labor market accelerates at the rate my seatmate predicted, it will soon become a very concrete certainty. Vast areas of the country will be on the dole, with no hope of ever getting off it. We know what happens when a middle class realizes that its hopes have been betrayed, that the system no longer works, that political leaders no longer know how to shelter it from catastrophe. Middle-class people look around for a scapegoat—somebody to blame for a catastrophe which they themselves did nothing to deserve.

In Germany, the scapegoats for the Depression were the Jews. In the Germany of the early twenty-first century, they will probably be from Southern or Eastern Europe, since there are no more Jews left to kill. In France they will probably be Algerian and Moroccan immigrants. In the America of that period, the scapegoats will presumably be, as usual, African-Americans. Race will matter even more than it does now. The color of one's skin will be even more a matter of life and death than at present.

The idea that Americans will see the need to tighten their belts, as my seatmate put it, would make sense if the country as a whole could resolve to tighten its belt—if we could do so consensually, as a community, in a way that ensured that nobody would profit from the new global economy at anybody else's expense. But this will not happen. The decision to tighten America's belt will not be made by the people, nor by their elected representatives. It will be the result of lots of small, unpublicized decisions, taken behind the scenes in boardrooms and offices.

The people who make these decisions will see no need to tighten their own personal belts. On the contrary, the managerial class will probably vote itself an increase, for their decision to globalize manufacturing will greatly improve their companies' bottom lines.

Indeed, it is not clear that the Americans at the top of the business community will, by that time, be thinking of themselves as having any particular attachment to the country of which they are citizens. They will have become citizens of the world. Their sources of capital, the majority of the people with whom they do deals, and the vast majority of their employees, may no longer be US citizens. They may have come to think of themselves as happily free from merely national interests as the giants of nineteenth-century American capitalism were free of merely state and local interests. They may become dismissive of the parochialism of people who, like Walt Whitman, John Dewey, James Baldwin, and Martin Luther King Jr., shared a national dream—people who still want, in Baldwin's phrase, to "achieve our country."

America held itself together and made moral progress in the twentieth century. It did not succumb to what the American Legion used to call "the warfare of the classes and the masses." This was because its white population formed a fairly well-integrated community of economic interest, one in which rising tides did in fact raise all boats. The disputes between management and labor were about slices of a pie which kept growing. At times even the descendants of the black slaves have been given a slightly larger share of that growing pie. But all bets, and all tacit social compacts, will be off if it ever becomes clear that the pie is going to keep right on shrinking. Not only may the US decide to repeal the civil rights revolution, it may give up on the whole idea of the American Dream. It may become a community of resentment rather than a community of hope, a community of vengeance rather than of reciprocal trust.

The only people who are in a position to know whether my and Luttwak's forecasts are too pessimistic are, once again, the leaders of the American business community—the people who make, or at least hear about, decisions on whether a factory will move from North Carolina to Slovenia, or on whether it is more profitable to have a product assembled in Thailand than in Virginia. I and my fellow academics do not know many of these people, and we do not have any idea how they see the moral situation in which they find themselves—nor even whether or not they see themselves as in an ethical dilemma.

We can only hope they do. For not only are these leaders the only people to have a perspicuous view of globalizing trends, they are the only people who might conceivably influence the country's thinking about how to deal with these trends. Our increasingly cynical political leaders are far too concerned with short-term reelection prospects to pay attention to the question of how much money Americans will be making twenty years from now, and how they will feel about making that amount of money. Just as the economic revolution which Luttwak believes to be going on is entirely a top-down phenomenon, concern for the sociopolitical effects of that revolution will be found, if anywhere, only at the top.

I have no idea whether the business community is prepared to think about the fate of the democracies in the next century, prepared to think about the sociopolitical consequences of economic globalization. But if they do not, I have no idea who will. Academics like Luttwak may shout or whimper from the sidelines, but it is hard to imagine that either the public or the politicians will take heed. Yet if the business leaders spoke as national leaders—if they were frank with the rest of us about the long-term prospects for our country—perhaps both the public and the politicians would notice that something important was going to happen, and start talking about it.

What I have said may seem to have little to do with concerns about race. But if we think about the relations between races in a global perspective and over a long term, there is an obvious relevance. The combination of high technology and free markets has been, for two hundred years, almost exclusively the property of white people, with the occasional crumbs tossed to others. But in the next century, the effect of this combination may be to redistribute economic opportunity without regard for race, to the vast relative deprivation of white people. The first beneficiaries of the distribution are obviously going to be Asian, but eventually factories may stop being sent from Virginia to Thailand and be sent to Nigeria or South Africa instead. This deprivation may strike the Third World as just what the white race deserves, but such resentment overlooks the fact that the white race used its money to create, among other things, free elections, a free judiciary, a free press, and free universities. It is far from clear that, if the white race grows too poor and desperate to support these institutions, they will spring up elsewhere.

However the Asians and the Africans fare, the African-Americans will almost certainly lose everything they have gained, and more. For the likely effect of the kind of lowering of white Americans' standard of living will be a recursion to the idea that it is outrageous that a white family should have little when a black family has much. It is not so long ago, after all, that when a black sharecropper had managed to buy a mule, his muleless white neighbor would shoot that mule. The white man shot the mule in order to preserve the natural order of things, the order of things ordained by God.

If Luttwak's scenario comes true, the suburban black middle class of the United States might conceivably manage to survive, with blacks and white in the suburbs commiserating with each other at PTA meetings on the hard times, and agreeing that the country needs a strong leader. But I would bet that things will get unimaginably worse for the blacks in the cities, simply because our new strong leaders will have to take out the country's resentment on somebody, and urban black men will be the obvious choice. Already the national, state, and local governments have arranged things so that urban blacks live largely outside the protection of the laws. They live in blocks which the police dare not enter, and in circumstances in which crime is often the only practicable career option. If jobs continue to be drained from the country, "crime" will be used as a euphemism for "the blacks," and the war on crime will become indistinguishable from a race war. Already many African-Americans believe that the government's failure to remove drugs and handguns from circulation is a white conspiracy against them—a way of making sure that black men destroy each other, rather than burdening either the labor market or the welfare rolls. Whether or not this is true now, it may become the evident fact of the future.

Let me end by returning to the question of whether the American business community will put business or America first. My hunch is that that decision is the most momentous and salient question of business ethics on the horizon. I have nothing to offer in refutation of the usual arguments for NAFTA, GATT, and free trade generally—nor against my seatmate's thesis that labor too is a commodity. But I also have nothing to offer to offset Luttwak's argument that globalization of the labor market will mean the end of democratic government in the rich, fat, lazy, overpaid, white countries which invented such government. I have no answers, only questions, and the hope that the business community is thinking about those questions.

When I am at my most pessimistic, however, I lose even that hope. George Orwell wrote that "since the end of the Neolithic Age, there have been three kinds of people in the world, the High, the Middle and the Low." "The aim of the High," he continued, "is to remain where they are. The aim of the Middle is to change places with the High. The aim of the Low, when they have an aim—for it is an abiding characteristic of the Low that they are too much crushed by drudgery to be more than intermittently conscious of anything outside their daily lives—is to abolish all distinctions and to create a society in which all men shall be equal."[2]

The Western Europeans created, late in our century, and for the first time in human history, societies in which the distinction between the Middle and the Low almost, though not quite, disappeared. They falsified, at least for a time, Marx's prediction of the progressive immiseration of the proletariat. We Americans had created, by the middle of the century, a society in which the distinction between the Middle and the Low almost disappeared from within the white majority. It was preserved only in the form of a hereditary caste distinction between black and white.

The globalization of the labor market seems likely to tear the white population of the United States apart once again; one result may be the expatriation of the American representatives of the High to villas in Switzerland, or beach houses in the suburbs of Singapore. The High may become citizens of the world, a supernational superclass which prides itself on being above both national and racial allegiance. What makes me most pessimistic is the thought that the tightening of American belts, and the consequent end of democratic government, may mean almost nothing to the High, even though it will mean everything to the American Dream of a society in which all men and women are equal. I hope that I am completely wrong about this, but this conference[3] seemed a good occasion to offer my fears, and my pessimism, as topics for discussion.

11

BACK TO CLASS POLITICS

(1997)

If you go to Britain and attend a Labor Party rally, you will probably hear the audience sing "The Red Flag." That song begins,
"The people's flag is deepest red. It's shrouded oft our martyred
dead. But ere their limbs grew stiff and cold, Their hearts' blood
dyed its every fold."

You may find this song maudlin and melodramatic. But it
will remind you of something that many people have forgotten:
that the history of the labor unions, in Britain, America, and
everywhere else in the world, is a blood-drenched history of
violent struggle. Like the civil rights movement, the labor
movement owed its successes to repeated and deliberate criminal acts—acts which we now think of as heroic civil disobedience, but which were brutally punished. To obstruct scabs from
entering a workplace into which they are invited by the owners
of that workplace is a criminal act, just as it is a criminal act to
sit in at a lunch-counter after the proprietor asks you to leave.
The police who brutalized the strikers thought of themselves as
preventing criminal acts from taking place, and they were right.
But, of course, the strikers were also right when they replied

that the police were acting as the agents of employers who refused to give their workers a decent share of the value those workers produced. To persuade the American people to see strikes, and violence against strikers, in this alternative way took a very long time. Only after an enormous amount of suffering, and very gradually, did it become politically impossible for mayors, governors, and sheriffs to send in their men to break strikers' skulls. Only in recent years has this strategy once again become politically possible.

We are accustomed to seeing labor leaders photographed with presidents, and officials of General Motors and of the United Auto Workers jumping up and shaking hands at the end of a successful bargaining session. So we think of labor unions as fine old American institutions, built into the fabric of the country. We think of strikes as an accepted, and perfectly reasonable, method of bringing about a slightly fairer distribution of profits. But we should remember that the early history of labor unions in America, as in the rest of the world, is a history of the skulls of strikers being broken by truncheons, decade after decade. We should also realize that those truncheons have recently reappeared: as John Sweeney reminds us in his book, during the last few years they have been used on striking janitors in Los Angeles and striking coal miners in Virginia.[1]

We should also remember that the history of the labor movement is one of heroic self-deprivation. Only after a great many striking mothers had seen their children go hungry were the unions able to accumulate enough money to set up strike funds, and to provide a little help. Only because millions of workers refused to become scabs by taking jobs which would have meant food for their families did the strikes eventually succeed. You would never guess, from Amitai Etzioni's, William Bennett's, and Robert Bork's writings about the need to overcome liberal individualism, that the labor unions provide by far the best examples in America's history of the virtues which these writers claim we must recapture. The history of the unions provides the best examples of comradeship, loyalty, and self-sacrifice.

Sometimes American unions have become corrupt, and have been taken over by greedy and cynical crooks. In this respect, their record is no better or worse than that of American churches, American law firms, American business firms, and even American academic departments. But at their best, the labor unions are America at its best. Like the civil rights movement, the union movement is a paradigm case of Americans getting together on their own and changing society from the bottom up—forcing it to become more decent, more democratic, and more humane. The strikers who braved the wrath of the police and the National Guard created a moral atmosphere in which no one was willing to be seen crossing a picket line, or be caught wearing clothes that did not bear a union label, or be known to have scabbed. This unwillingness was an expression of the sort of human solidarity which made the year 1989 possible in Eastern Europe, and which made the Founding Fathers willing to risk their lives, their fortunes, and their sacred honor. The fact that people are now once again willing to cross picket lines, and are unwilling to ask themselves who makes their clothes or who picks their vegetables, is a symptom of moral decline.

Most American schoolchildren learn something about the martyrs of the civil rights movement. They at least know how Martin Luther King Jr. died. Perhaps they have also heard of Medgar Evans or of Andrew Goodman. But these schoolchildren usually have no idea of how it came about that most American workers have an eight-hour day and a five-day work week. They are unlikely to be taught about the conditions in the sweatshops and factories in which their great-grandparents worked, nor about how the unions made those conditions a little better for their grandparents and parents. They know nothing of the blood that had to be spilled, and the hunger that had to be endured, in order that unions could be transformed from criminal conspiracies into fine old American institutions.

We should help our students understand that social justice in America has owed much more to civil disobedience than to the use of the ballot. The students need to know that the deepest and most enduring injustices, like the unending humiliation of African-Americans and the miserable wages paid to unorganized workers, are always downplayed by the political parties, and by most of the press. They need to remember that the same argument now used against raising the minimum wage—that doing so will discourage economic efficiency and productivity—was once used against the eight-hour day. They need to be able to spot the resemblances between what the politicians were indirectly and gently bribed to ignore at the beginning of this century and what they are being indirectly and gently bribed to ignore now. They need to realize that the last hundred years of our country's history has witnessed a brutal struggle between the corporations and the workers, that this struggle is still going on, and that the corporations are winning. They need to know that the deepest social problems usually go unmentioned by candidates for political office, because it is not in the interest of the rich to have those problems discussed in public.

Today our country, like the other industrialized democracies, faces a problem that few politicians, except for scurrilous fascists like Pat Buchanan and, in France, Jean-Marie Le Pen, seem willing to talk about: the wages of European and American workers are ridiculously high by world standards. There is less and less need to employ any of these workers, since the same work can be done elsewhere for a fifth of the cost. Furthermore, the globalization of the markets in capital and labor means that no nation's economy is sufficiently self-contained to permit long-term social planning by a national government. So the American economy is passing out of the control of the American government, and thus out of the control of the American voters.

This new situation is fine with the 1 percent of Americans who own 40 percent of their country's wealth. Their dividends typically increase when jobs are exported from Ohio to South China, and from North Carolina to Thailand. The strength of the dollar does not matter to them, because their investment advisors can flip their money into other currencies at the touch of a button. They have less and less at stake in America's future, and more and more invested in an efficient and productive global economy—an economy made ever more efficient and productive by the constant expansion of the global labor market into poorer and poorer countries. There is little reason to believe that what is good for GM, or Microsoft, is good for America. The economic royalists whom Franklin Roosevelt denounced still had a lot invested in America's future. For today's superrich, such an investment would be imprudent.

There is much too little public discussion of the changes which this globalized labor market will inevitably bring to America in the coming decades. Bill Bradley is one of the few prominent politicians to have insisted that we must prevent our country breaking up into hereditary economic castes. Writers like Michael Lind and Edward Luttwak are sketching very plausible scenarios of an America in which the top fifth of the country, the well-educated professionals, carry out the orders of the international superrich. These people will get paid between $75,000 and $500,000 a year to do so. The remaining four-fifths of the country, the four-fifths which now has a median family income of $30,000, will get a little less in every successive year, and will keep on doing all the dirty work. America, the country which was to have witnessed a new birth of freedom, will gradually be divided by class differences of a sort which would have utterly inconceivable to Jefferson, or to Lincoln, or to Walt Whitman.

Unless the politicians begin to talk about long-term social planning, Lind and Luttwak argue, economic inequality, and the formation of hereditary economic castes, will continue unchecked. Maybe these authors are too pessimistic, but we shall never know unless the questions they pose are taken up by candidates for public office. The most important single reason for hoping that American labor unions will become much bigger and more powerful than they are now is that they are the only organizations who want to get these questions on the table—to force politicians to talk about what is going to happen to wages, and how we are going to avoid increasing economic injustice. If a revived union movement could get out the vote in the old mill towns, in the rural slums, and in the inner cities, instead of letting the suburban vote set the national political agenda, those questions would be on the table.

The whole point of America was that it was going to be the world's first classless society. It was going to be a place where janitors, executives, professors, nurses, and salesclerks would look each other in the eye, and respect each other as fellow-citizens. It was going to be a place where their kids all went to the same schools, and where they got the same treatment from the police and the courts. From the days of Franklin Roosevelt to those of Lyndon Johnson, we made enormous progress toward the creation of such a society. In the twenty years between World War II and Vietnam, the newly respectable labor unions made their presence felt on the national scene, and accomplished a great deal. Those were the years in which academics like

Daniel Bell, Arthur Schlesinger, and John Kenneth Galbraith worked side by side with labor leaders like Walter Reuther and A. Philip Randolph.

The Vietnam War saw the end of the traditional alliance between the academics and the unions—an alliance which had nudged the Democratic party steadily to the left during the previous twenty years. We are still living with the consequences of the anti–Vietnam War movement, and in particular with those of the rage of the increasingly manic student protesters of the late 1960s. These protesters were absolutely right that Vietnam was an unjust war, a massacre of which our country will always be ashamed. But when the students began to burn flags, and to spit at returning soldiers, they did deeper and more long-lasting damage to the American left than they could ever have imagined. When they began to spell "America" with a "k," they lost the respect and the sympathy of the union members. Until George McGovern's defeat in 1972, the New Left did not realize that it had unthinkingly destroyed an alliance which had been central to American leftist politics.

Since those days, leftists in the colleges and universities have concentrated their energies on academic politics rather than on national politics. As Todd Gitlin put it, we academics marched on the English department while the Republicans took over the White House. While we had our backs turned, the labor unions were being steadily ground down by the shift to a service economy, and by the machinations of the Reagan and Bush administrations. The best thing that could happen to the American left would be for the academics to get back into the class struggle, and for the labor union members to forgive and forget the stupid and self-defeating anti-American rhetoric which filled the universities of the late 1960s.

This is not to say that those twenty-five years of inward-looking academic politics were in vain. American campuses are very much better places—*morally* better places—than they were in 1970. Thanks to all those marches on the English department, and various other departments, the situation of women, gays, lesbians, African-Americans, and Hispanics has been enormously improved. Their new role in the academy is helping improve their situation in the rest of American society.

Nevertheless, leftist academic politics has run its course. It is time to revive the kind of leftist politics which pervaded American campuses from the Great Depression through the early 1960s—a politics which centers on the struggle to prevent the rich from ripping off the rest of the country. If the unions will help us revive this kind of politics, maybe the academy and the labor movement can get together again. Maybe together we can help bring our country closer to the goal which matters most: the classless society. That is the cause for which the AFL-CIO organizers are now fighting, and for which some of their predecessors died.

12

MAKING THE RICH RICHER

(2000)

A few days ago, I got a nice letter from the Social Security Administration, telling me that I was entitled to some $1,600 a month, but that unfortunately I couldn't receive it because I was still earning a lot of money. Last week I opened the newspaper to find that the House of Representatives has voted unanimously to have the money sent to me anyway. The Senate and the president, it appears, are quite prepared to approve this change. So in the course of this year I shall get government checks for about $20,000. About $8,000 of it will go for federal and state taxes, but I shall still have a net $1,000 extra a month that I never expected to have.

I do not feel entitled to that money. Like a lot of other Americans who are sixty-eight, I am making a very good living. When I stop working, I will get a pension that ensures that I still live perfectly comfortably. I would like Congress to use the Social Security taxes I've paid over the last forty-five years to promote the general welfare.

That means leveling things out a bit, so that my fellow sixty-eight-year-olds who could not go to college, and could not get nice, highly paid, white-collar jobs like mine, will have a better chance at a reasonably comfortable old age. Congress could have sent the extra money it wants to send me, and millions like me, to some of my fellow sexagenarians who do need it. These include all those arthritic sixty-eight-year-olds who are shelving groceries, or standing on their feet all day making change, for $7 an hour. They are doing this because their monthly Social Security payments will probably never rise above $1,000.

Members of Congress know perfectly well that the rich have been getting steadily richer and the poor poorer—that Americans like me are getting a bigger and bigger share of the gross national product, whereas the people who clean the toilets in my office building are getting less and less of it. But this knowledge seems to have no influence on them whatever. They act as if promoting the general welfare meant promoting the interest of people who make more than $50,000 a year. As Nicholas von Hoffman has put it, we live under "government of the comfortable, by the comfortable and for the comfortable."

Once the boom stops, and the Silicon Valley bubble bursts, we can expect our elected representatives to take considerable pains to see that the comfortable remain comfortable, while letting the poor assume any burdens that must be borne. The man who puts in eight hours making sandwiches at a cafeteria on the Stanford campus, and another eight hours bringing glasses of ever fruitier cabernet and ever spicier chardonnay to us comfortably off folk in one of Palo Alto's better restaurants, will probably lose his second job, because many of the professionals in Silicon Valley will start drinking jug wine at home.

This will probably mean that this man cannot move his kids into a school district where they might learn something, and that they will never get properly educated. Our elected representatives can be expected to look with equanimity on this steady reinforcement of our present system of hereditary castes.

President Clinton has said that he will sign the legislation that gives me that extra $1,000 a month. He should think again. He is a decent and generous-spirited man, whose attempts to do the right thing have been frustrated by Republican majorities in Congress. But he could use his last year in office to speak out. With the backing of Vice-President Al Gore and former Senator Bill Bradley, he could ask Congress to take the bill back and make it a little less absurd—a little more fair, a little less selfish.

Our president has been good at political compromises, but unless he takes a few uncompromising stands before leaving office he will go down in history as having acquiesced in our nation's moral decline. This decline has nothing to do with our sexual mores. It has everything to do with our increasing willingness to let the rich take more and more from the poor.

13

LOOKING BACKWARDS FROM
THE YEAR 2096

(1996)

Our long, hesitant, painful recovery, over the last five decades, from the breakdown of democratic institutions during the Dark Years (2014–2044) has changed our political vocabulary, as well as our sense of the relation between the moral order and the economic order. Just as twentieth-century Americans had trouble imagining how their pre–Civil War ancestors could have stomached slavery, so we at the end of the twenty-first century have trouble imagining how our great-grandparents could have legally permitted a CEO to get twenty times more than her lowest-paid employees. We cannot understand how Americans a hundred years ago could have tolerated the horrific contrast between a childhood spent in the suburbs and one spent in the ghettos. Such inequalities seem to us evident moral abominations, but the vast majority of our ancestors took them to be regrettable necessities.

As long as their political discourse was dominated by the notion of "rights"—whether "individual" or "civil"—it was hard for Americans to think of the results of unequal distribution of wealth and income as immoral. Such rights talk, common among late twentieth-century liberals, gave conservative opponents of redistributionist policies a tremendous advantage: "the right to a job" (or "to a decent wage") had none of the resonance of "the right to sit in the front of the bus" or "the right to vote" or even "the right to equal pay for equal work." Rights in the liberal tradition were, after all, powers and privileges to be wrested from the state, not from the economy.

Of course, socialists had, since the mid-nineteenth century, urged that the economy and the state be merged to guarantee economic rights. But it had become clear by the middle of the twentieth century that such merging was disastrous. The history of the pre-1989 "socialist" countries—bloody dictatorships that paid only lip service to the fraternity for which the socialist revolutionaries had yearned—made it plausible for conservatives to argue that extending the notion of rights to the economic order would be a step down the road to serfdom. By the end of the twentieth century, even left-leaning American intellectuals agreed that "socialism, no wave of the future, now looks (at best) like a temporary historical stage through which various nations passed before reaching the great transition to capitalist democracy."[1]

The realization by those on the left that a viable economy required free markets did not stop them from insisting that capitalism would be compatible with American ideals of human brotherhood only if the state were able to redistribute wealth. Yet this view was still being criticized as "un-American" and "socialist" at the beginning of the present century, even as, under the pressures of a globalized world economy, the gap between most Americans' incomes and those of the lucky one-third at the top widened. Looking back, we think how easy it would have been for our great-grandfathers to have forestalled the social collapse that resulted from these economic pressures. They could have insisted that all classes had to confront the new global economy together. In the name of our common citizenship, they could have asked everybody, not just the bottom two-thirds, to tighten their belts and make do with less. They might have brought the country together by bringing back its old pride in fraternal ideals.

But as it happened, decades of despair and horror were required to impress Americans with lessons that now seem blindingly obvious.

The apparent incompatibility of capitalism and democracy is, of course, an old theme in American political and intellectual life. It began to be sounded more than two centuries ago. Historians divide our history into the hundred years before the coming of industrial capitalism and the more than two hundred years since. During the first period, the open frontier made it possible for Americans to live in ways that became impossible for their descendants. If you were white in nineteenth-century America, you always had a second chance: something was always opening up out West.

So the first fault line in American politics was not between the rich and the poor. Instead, it was between those who saw chattel slavery as incompatible with American fraternity and those who did not. (Abolitionist posters showed a kneeling slave asking, "Am I not a man, and a brother?") But only forty years after the Civil War, reformers were already saying that the problem of chattel slavery had been replaced by that of wage slavery.

The urgency of that problem dominates Herbert Croly's progressivist manifesto of 1909, *The Promise of American Life*. Croly argued that the Constitution, and a tradition of tolerant individualism, had kept America hopeful and filled with what he called "genuine good-fellowship" during its first hundred years.

But beginning with the first wave of industrialization in the 1870s and 1880s, things began to change. Wage slavery—a life of misery and toil, without a sense of participation in the national life, and without any trace of the frontiersman's proud independence—became the fate of more and more Americans. Alexis de Tocqueville had rejoiced that an opulent merchant and his shoemaker, when they met on the streets of Philadelphia in 1840, would exchange political opinions. "These two citizens," he wrote, "are concerned with affairs of state and they do not part without shaking hands."[2] Croly feared that this kind of unforced fraternity was becoming impossible.

From Croly to John Kenneth Galbraith and Arthur Schlesinger in the 1960s, reformers urged that we needed some form of redistribution to bring back Tocquevillian comity. They battled with conservatives who claimed that redistributive measures would kill economic prosperity. The reformers insisted that what Theodore Roosevelt had called "the money power" and Dwight Eisenhower "the military-industrial complex" was the true enemy of American ideals. The conservatives rejoined that the only enemy of democracy was the state and that the economy must be shielded from do-gooders.

This debate simmered through the first two decades following the Second World War. During that relatively halcyon period, most Americans could get fairly secure, fairly well-paying jobs and could count on their children having a better life than theirs. White America seemed to be making slow but steady progress toward a classless society. Only the growth of the increasingly miserable black underclass reminded white Americans that the promise of American life was still far from being fulfilled.

The sense that this promise was still alive was made possible, in part, by what the first edition of this *Companion* called the "rights revolution." Most of the moral progress that took place in the second half of the twentieth century was brought about by the Supreme Court's invocation of constitutional rights, in such decisions as *Brown v. Board of Education* (1954) and *Romer v. Evans* (1996), the first Supreme Court decision favorable to homosexuals. But this progress was confined almost entirely to improvements in the situation of groups identified by race, ethnicity, or sexuality. The situation of women and of homosexuals changed radically in this period. Indeed, it is now clear that those changes, which spread from America around the world, were the most lasting and significant moral achievements of the twentieth century.

But though such groups could use the rhetoric of rights to good effect, the trade unions, the unemployed, and those employed at the ludicrously low minimum wage ($174 an hour, in 2095 dollars, compared with the present minimum of $400) could not. Perhaps no difference between present-day American political discourse and that of one hundred years ago is greater than our assumption that the first duty of the state is to prevent gross economic and social inequality, as opposed to our ancestors' assumption that the government's only moral duty was to ensure "equal protection of the laws"—laws that, in their majestic impartiality, allowed the rich and the poor to receive the same hospital bills.

The Supreme Court, invoking this idea of equal protection, began the great moral revival we know as the civil rights movement. The *Brown* decision initiated both an explosion of violence and an upsurge of fraternal feeling. Some white Americans burned crosses and black churches. Many more had their eyes opened to the humiliations being inflicted on their fellow citizens: if they did not join civil rights marches, they at least felt relieved of guilt when the Court threw out miscegenation laws and when Congress began to protect black voting rights.

For a decade or so there was an uplifting sense of moral improvement. For the first time, white and black Americans started to think of each other as fellow citizens.

By the beginning of the 1980s, however, this sense of fraternity was only a faint memory. A burst of selfishness had produced tax revolts in the 1970s, stopping in its tracks the fairly steady progress toward a full-fledged welfare state that had been under way since the New Deal. The focus of racial hate was transferred from the rural South to the big cities, where a criminal culture of unemployed (and, in the second generation, virtually unemployable) black youths grew up—a culture of near constant violence, made possible by the then-famous American "right to bear arms." All the old racial prejudices were revived by white suburbanites' claims that their tax money was being used to coddle criminals. Politicians gained votes by promising to spend what little money could be squeezed from their constituents on prisons rather than on day care.

Tensions between the comfortable middle-class suburbs and the rest of the country grew steadily in the closing decades of the twentieth century, as the gap between the educated and well paid and the uneducated and ill paid steadily widened. Class division came into existence between those who made "professional" salaries and those whose hourly wage kept sinking toward the minimum. But the politicians pretended to be unaware of this steady breakdown of fraternity.

Our nation's leaders, in the last decade of the old century and the first of the new, seemed never to have thought that it might be dangerous to make automatic weapons freely and cheaply available to desperate men and women—people without hope—living next to the centers of transportation and communication. Those weapons burst into the streets in 2014, in the revolution that, leaving the cities in ruins and dislocating

American economic life, plunged the country into the Second Great Depression. The insurgency in the ghettos, coming at a time when all but the wealthiest Americans felt desperately insecure, led to the collapse of trust in government. The collapse of the economy produced a war of all against all, as gasoline and food became harder and harder to buy, and as even the suburbanites began to brandish guns at their neighbors. As the generals never stopped saying throughout the Dark Years, only the military saved the country from utter chaos.

Here, in the late twenty-first century, as talk of fraternity and unselfishness has replaced talk of rights, American political discourse has come to be dominated by quotations from Scripture and literature, rather than from political theorists or social scientists. Fraternity, like friendship, was not a concept that either philosophers or lawyers knew how to handle. They could formulate principles of justice, equality, and liberty, and invoke these principles when weighing hard moral or legal issues. But how to formulate a "principle of fraternity"? Fraternity is an inclination of the heart, one that produces a sense of shame at having much when others have little. It is not the sort of thing that anybody can have a theory about or that people can be argued into having.

Perhaps the most vivid description of the American concept of fraternity is found in a passage from John Steinbeck's 1939 novel, *The Grapes of Wrath*. Steinbeck describes a desperately impoverished family, dispossessed tenant farmers from Oklahoma, camped out at the edge of Highway 66, sharing their food with an even more desperate migrant family. Steinbeck writes, "'I have a little food' plus 'I have none.' If from this problem the sum is 'We have a little food,' the movement has direction." As long as people in trouble can sacrifice to help people who are in still worse trouble, Steinbeck insisted, there is fraternity, and therefore social hope.

The movement Steinbeck had in mind was the revolutionary socialism that he, like many other leftists of the 1930s, thought would be required to bring the First Great Depression to an end. "The quality of owning," he wrote, "freezes you forever into the 'I,' and cuts you off forever from the 'we.'" Late twentieth-century liberals no longer believed in getting rid of private ownership, but they agreed that the promise of American life could be redeemed only as long as Americans were willing to sacrifice for the sake of fellow Americans—only as long as they could see the government not as stealing their tax money but as needing it to prevent unnecessary suffering.

The Democratic Vistas Party, the coalition of trade unions and churches that toppled the military dictatorship in 2044, has retained control of Congress by successfully convincing the voters that its opponents constitute "the parties of selfishness." The traditional use of "brother" and "sister" in union locals and religious congregations is the principal reason why "fraternity" (or, among purists, "siblinghood") is now the name of our most cherished ideal.

In the first two centuries of American history, Jefferson's use of rights had set the tone for political discourse, but now political argument is not about who has the right to what but about what can best prevent the reemergence of hereditary castes—either racial or economic. The old union slogan "An injury to one is an injury to all" is now the catchphrase of American politics. "Solidarity Forever" and "This Land Is Your Land" are sung at least as often as "The Star-Spangled Banner."

Until the last fifty years, moral instruction in America had inculcated personal responsibility, and most sermons had focused on individual salvation. Today morality is thought of neither as a matter of applying the moral law nor as the acquisition of virtues but as fellow feeling, the ability to sympathize with the plight of others.

In the churches, the "social gospel" theology of the early twentieth century has been rediscovered. Walter Rauschenbusch's "Prayer against the servants of Mammon" ("Behold the servants of Mammon, who defy thee and drain their fellowmen for gain . . . who have made us ashamed of our dear country by their defilements and have turned our holy freedom into a hollow name") is familiar to most churchgoers. In the schools, students learn about our country's history from social novels describing our past failures to hang together when we needed to, the novels of Steinbeck, Upton Sinclair, Theodore Dreiser, Richard Wright, and, of course, Russell Banks's samizdat novel, *Trampling the Vineyards* (2021).

Historians unite in calling the twentieth the "American" century. Certainly it was in the twentieth century that the United States was richest, most powerful, most influential, and most self-confident. Our ancestors one hundred years ago still thought of the country as destined to police, inform, and inspire the world. Compared with the Americans of one hundred years ago, we are citizens of an isolationist, unambitious, middle-grade nation.

Our products are only now becoming competitive again in international markets, and Democratic Vistas politicians continue to urge that our consistently low productivity is a small price to pay for union control of the workplace and worker ownership of the majority of firms. We continue to lag behind the European Community, which was able to withstand the pressures of a globalized labor market by having a full-fledged welfare state already in place, and which (except for Austria and Great Britain) was able to resist the temptation to impoverish the most vulnerable in order to keep its suburbanites affluent. Spared the equivalent of our own Dark Years, Europe still, despite all that China can do, holds the position we lost in 2014: it still dominates both the world's economy and its culture.

For two centuries, Americans believed that they were as far ahead of Europe, in both virtue and promise, as Europe was ahead of the rest of the world. But American exceptionalism did not survive the Dark Years: we no longer think of ourselves as singled out by divine favor. We are now, once again, a constitutional democracy, but we have proved as vulnerable as Germany, Russia, and India to dictatorial takeovers. We have a sense of fragility, of susceptibility to the vicissitudes of time and chance, which Walt Whitman and John Dewey may never have known.

Perhaps no American writer will ever again begin a book, as Croly did, by saying, "The faith of Americans in their own country is religious, if not in its intensity, at any rate in its almost absolute and universal authority." But our chastened mood, our lately learned humility, may have made us better able to realize that everything depends on keeping our fragile sense of American fraternity intact.

III

GLOBAL POLITICS

14

THE UNPREDICTABLE AMERICAN EMPIRE

(2003)

As Michael Ignatieff has pointed out, a country that has military bases around the world, commands military force capable of overwhelming any opponent, displays increasing arrogance in its attitude toward other nations, and sees international agreements and institutions as tools to be manipulated in its own interests, can plausibly be described as an "empire."[1] Still, the contrast between empire and republic can be misleading. For when we think of the transition from the Roman Republic to the Roman Empire, we think of two quite different things—the imposition of the *pax Romana* on places far away from the imperial capital, and an increasingly authoritarian internal regime.

The United States, like the Roman Republic, is a corrupt plutocracy, but it is not an authoritarian regime. It is still a constitutional democracy in which elections make a difference. The press and the universities are free, and the judiciary remains independent. The world is lucky that the country that serves as a global policeman—the one that guarantees the counterpart of the *pax Romana*—is not yet one in which an autocrat can do whatever he likes.

Under the bad caesars, the only remedy was the assassination of the tyrant. In the United States, a bad president can still be removed by the decision of the electorate. There is still plenty of internal debate going on in the United States about how to play our policing role and whether and how to try to shift this role to the United Nations. The appalling document published by the Bush administration—"The National Security Strategy of the United States of America"—would not have been issued by a Gore administration, and Gore would have been elected had he received the three million votes that American leftists gave to Ralph Nader.

The rest of the world should not think that someone like Bush—an ignorant and arrogant president, without either internationalist ideals or an aspiration for social justice—is the inevitable consequence of America's rise to unchallenged hegemony. He is just a piece of very bad luck. But of course he also represents a very great danger. If there are further successful terrorist attacks on the scale of 9/11, the Bush administration will almost certainly use them as an excuse to put the country under what amounts to martial law. This administration has no respect for civil liberties and would cheerfully turn the FBI into a Gestapo if it thought it could get away with it.

Even if there are no new terrorist attacks, the United States may well become even more of a garrison state than it already is. If future decisions on foreign policy are made by as small a cabal as the one that decided to invade Iraq, then the United States will remain a republic only in a very tenuous sense. If we see a series of Republican administrations and of Republican-dominated Congresses stretching over the next two decades, the American public will probably become accustomed to seeing our military forces suddenly dispatched abroad for reasons that are even vaguer and more confusing than those that were used as a rationale for the Iraq War. The opinions of the Democratic minority in Congress and of the liberal media (the *New York Times*, for example) will be brushed aside without a thought, and without the courtesy of a response, by Republican chieftains who think the affairs of the world too important to be entrusted to the judgment of the electorate.

If this pessimistic scenario were to play out, then the parallel with Rome would become complete. The shift from constitutional democracy to autocracy can become irreversible before anybody quite realizes that it is taking place. If the Democratic Party gradually ceases to function as a counterweight to bellicose White House cabals, historians may someday compare the "splitter" role of Ralph Nader's Green Party in 2000 to the refusal of the Communists to make common cause with the Social Democrats in Germany in 1932.

My topic in this paper, however, is not the current situation. Rather, I want to go back over some of the ground covered in my book *Achieving Our Country*,[2] and to describe the split between two self-images of the United States that have emerged in the decades since the 1960s. One of these self-images is of a republic that is always in danger, thanks to its ever-increasing wealth and power, of becoming an empire. The other is of a country that has always been imperial and hypocritical, one whose pretensions to moral worth have always been undeserved.

One convenient way to follow recent debates about the nature of the United States is looking at the academic discipline called "American Studies"—a discipline that is barely fifty years old. Within that discipline, a massive shift has occurred, one that has made a great difference in what American university students are told about the history and the nature of their country. There has been a change from a triumphalist, exceptionalist, and hopeful view of the United States to a depressed and skeptical view.

This shift in perspective is the central topic of a much-cited essay by Gene Wise, "'Paradigm Dramas' in American Studies."[3] On Wise's account, which perfectly fits my own memories, most American intellectuals prior to the 1960s took for granted what he calls "the Parrington paradigm." Those who did so believed that there was such a thing as the American Mind, and that it was importantly different from the European Mind. This earlier generation took for granted that American thinkers and poets had long since done what Emerson hoped they might do: ceased to listen to "the courtly muses of Europe" and become inspired instead by "the spirit of American freedom." They agreed with Whitman that "Americans of all nations at any time upon the earth have probably the fullest poetical natures." They looked with scorn on the huge colonial empires that the European powers had grabbed in the course of the nineteenth century. Conveniently forgetting the Mexican-American War, they thought that their country's virtue was demonstrated by its having been content, at the end of the Spanish-American War, with very modest spoils.

These pre-1960s intellectuals also took for granted that their forefathers had brought forth upon the American continent a new birth of freedom, just as Lincoln had said. They saw the oppression of American workers by American capitalists and of American blacks by American whites as a tragic, but corrigible, failure to live up to ideals that remained central to the nation's self-image. They thought of the aggressive expansionism of the Mexican-American War, and of the annexation of Puerto Rico and the occupation of the Philippines at the beginning of the twentieth century, as unfortunate but long-past episodes—events that were not really important to the nation's story.

Many of the pre-1960s intellectuals I am describing called themselves socialists, but few of them were Marxists. Most of them thought the New Deal had shown that violent social revolution was unnecessary, and that social justice at home, like decolonialization abroad, could be brought about by gradual, step-by-step, top-down measures. All of them, white as well as black, were angry at the humiliation and misery still being inflicted on African-Americans, but they assumed that this problem, like that of poverty, could be solved by federal legislation.

Up until the mid-1960s, I wholeheartedly shared all the assumptions and attitudes I have been sketching. The people among whom I was brought up, and who shaped my political consciousness, knew very well, and helped publicize, what American whites were doing to American blacks. They also knew how viciously the bosses were still fighting the labor unions and how easy the rich found it to corrupt the American government. They agreed with Mencken and Veblen about the sad vulgarization of American middle-class life. Nevertheless, they did not doubt that the United States was the greatest and freest country that had ever existed. When Stalinist intellectuals defended the gulag by asking, "What about the lynchings of blacks in the United States?" these people replied that there was no comparison between a free country stained with racial hatred and a cruel tyranny. They conducted the struggle to make America a more just society in a spirit of sentimental patriotism. They regarded Gore Vidal's claim that we were rapidly moving from republic to empire as hysterical overstatement.

Things changed in the mid-1960s as more and more troops were sent to fight more and more hopeless battles against the Viet Cong. As Wise's article reminds us, the great post–World War II expansion of American higher education meant that most of the people of my generation who would, in my parents' generation, have become freelance writers and literary bohemians, became professors instead. So by 1965 almost every intellectual in the United States found himself teaching students who were quite likely to be drafted out of the classroom and sent off to fight in the jungles of Southeast Asia.

This created problems for those of us who wanted to be both patriots and social critics. The wars we and our parents had lived through—World Wars I and II—seemed to us to have been good, just wars. So, up until Vietnam, had the Cold War. The bad wars the United States had fought—the Mexican-American and Spanish-American Wars—were for us just memories of what the United States had been like in the bad old days before FDR. So to find our country once again waging a patently bad, unjust war made us question the faith in which we had grown up.

As people like me gradually realized both that the Vietnam War could not be won and that our government seemed nevertheless prepared to wage it forever, our image of our own nation began to change. We began to wonder how it must look not only in the eyes of our draft-age students, but in the eyes of the Vietnamese villagers we were napalming. This led us to realize how the United States had looked to Latin Americans ever since the CIA, in 1952, overthrew a left-wing Guatemalan government whose policies might have endangered the profits of the United Fruit Company. We began to see the Cold War, not just as a great and necessary crusade, but as a process that had subtly and silently corrupted our country from within. What Wise says about teachers of American Studies in this period—that they felt they must "assume an adversary role against the culture"—was true of many other academics, particularly those teaching in the social sciences and the humanities.

There was, however, a split between those who thought that the adversary was simply the American government of the moment and those who thought it was something deeper and more entrenched—the culture. We professors who had taken part in Martin Luther King Jr.'s civil rights march on Washington in 1963 and who by 1968 were joining antiwar marches through the streets of New York City were divided into two camps. There were some who thought that the good old Emerson-Lincoln-Whitman-Dewey story about America had been hypocritical self-delusion. They began to describe the United States as a racist, sexist, imperialist nation. They read Marx and Marcuse, and they started telling their students that reform was obviously never going to work, that revolution was the only answer. But there were others, of whom I was one, who thought that the image of America as lighting the way to freedom and justice might still be preserved.

People in my camp continued to think of the Cold War as a justified crusade against an evil empire, but we were gradually forced to admit that prosecuting that war had caused the government to fall into the hands of what President Eisenhower called "the military-industrial complex." This realization did not cause us to repudiate our country or our culture. We did not think that the story of America needed to be retold. We simply wanted to take the country back from the Pentagon and the corporations. If America would return to its senses and live up to its glorious past, we thought, it could continue to prosecute the Cold War, but in ways that did not commit it to the support of despotisms run out of the American embassy.

Even Cold Warriors like myself have now come to admit that we are citizens of something more like an empire than like the republic Emerson described and Whitman hymned. We still hope that the people might someday recapture the government from the control of the military-industrial complex and that someday our country will cease to be a garrison state. But we have to acknowledge that vast areas of national life have been turned over to the so-called iron triangle that links corporations, the Pentagon, and the Senate and House Armed Services Committees. The Congress, heavily bribed and deeply corrupt, never seriously debates life-and-death issues such as nuclear disarmament any more than it shows genuine concern for the needs of the American poor. It never discusses what to do about America's role in the international arms trade. That is why the collapse of the Soviet Union made so little difference to defense expenditures, why we still have enough nuclear warheads to destroy civilization, and why President Bush can repudiate treaties without much public outcry.

Our radical colleagues agree with all this, but they think that recent changes have simply made it easier to see what America has always been like. They see the Vietnam War as continuous with the Mexican-American War and the occupation of the Philippines. On their view, the contempt for nonwhites that all three episodes revealed was of a piece with the racism that has always permeated American society. They see leftist reformers like myself as naive, desperately trying to preserve the Parrington paradigm in the face of the facts.

We reformists, however, think that the radicals' picture of America as pretty much irredeemable is just a way of evading questions about how to change our country for the better. The radicals rejoin that electing liberal Democrats rather than conservative Republicans will never make any real difference to the country's behavior. As they see it, we liberals are those who, long after the Roman Republic has been succeeded by the Roman Empire, still worried about who would become consul.

The split within the ranks of American intellectuals that I have been describing is epitomized in the contrast between the views of David Hollinger, perhaps our most eminent scholar of American intellectual history, and those of Nikhil Pal Singh, who teaches American Studies at New York University.

Hollinger is, like myself, a social democrat and an admirer of Dewey. He wants American intellectuals to pay less attention to identity politics and to think more about what political initiatives to support. In 1995 he published a book called *Postethnic America: Beyond Multiculturalism*, in which he tried to revive the pre-1960s idea of America as an inclusive, pluralist society.[4] His subtitle, "Beyond Multiculturalism," was in part a protest against the way in which the term "multiculturalism" had become the watchword of the radicals—the term used to describe their skepticism toward the very idea of "American culture."

Hollinger's book was of a piece with books published around the same time by Todd Gitlin, Arthur Schlesinger Jr., and myself.[5] All four of us argued that it was time to stop emphasizing diversity and conflict and to try to formulate a consensus around which leftist intellectuals and the public as a whole might rally. What the country needed, we said, was not identity politics but what Gitlin called "majoritarian" politics—that is, political activity aimed at winning elections, getting bills through Congress, and filing suits that would produce court decisions favorable to liberal causes. We wanted intellectuals to let up on criticism of the culture and switch to criticism of, and changes in, the laws and in administrative policies. In particular, we wanted the intellectuals to talk less about race and more about class, because we hoped that a political majority might be formed if poor white people and poor black people made common cause.

The opposing, radical point of view was laid out in a 1998 article by Nikhil Singh titled "Culture/Wars: Recoding Empire in an Age of Democracy."[6] This was a comprehensive and very thoughtful overview of the radical-vs.-liberal opposition in American intellectual life in the course of the last six or seven decades. In it, Singh set his face against the whole cluster of ideas and attitudes common to Schlesinger, Gitlin, Hollinger, and myself. He sees our efforts as reactionary. He urges specialists in American Studies not to be seduced into reaffirming a discredited "universalism."

Singh's central criticism of Hollinger's project is that the attempt to revive a patriotic sense of common citizenship is "mystificatory" in that it obscures both racial and class conflict. "The problem," Singh says, "is that the concept of universalism in this discussion remains too closely aligned with the idea of nationalism and especially with the achievement of a hegemonic social formation capable of transcending differences, social antagonisms, and divisions."

I agree with Singh when he says that "the epistemic, historical, moral and worldly political status of internalized/externalized exclusion and inequality, perpetuated by the civic nation, constitutes the proper, if vexed, terrain of the culture wars." But I disagree with him when he goes on to say, "In this conflictual, communal conversation, the reassertion of American universalism actually provides few solutions; it only begs more questions." It seems to me that the only thing that can provide solutions is a shared sense of citizenship, a sense of participation in a social formation capable of transcending differences, antagonisms, and divisions.

Singh and his fellow radicals think that any such sense of participation would be self-deceptive. Their point is that the rich and powerful whites who have manipulated American public opinion ever since the country's foundation created a series of fictions, including the fictions purveyed by Lincoln in the Gettysburg Address (a speech that all students in my elementary school were required to memorize). Singh and many other specialists in American Studies think that the principal task of scholars in this field is to debunk the Parringtonian and Lincol-nesque story of America as a land of freedom. Hollinger and those like him reply that the work of demystification has been accomplished, that we do not need to do it again and again, and that it is time to get back to consensus-building. Our central argument is that there is a difference between fictions and ide-als, and that you cannot have change for the better without an ideal to strive for.

To judge, by the content of *American Quarterly*, and in par-ticular by the tenor of recent presidential addresses to the American Studies Associations, Singh's point of view is now dominant among American academics who belong to that As-sociation. But Hollinger thinks, and I agree, that it would be a great misfortune for our country if our students were won over to Singh's way of thinking of the United States. On our view, one of the few things that might help ensure that we remain a republic would be the sense, in the rising generation, that our country's ideals have been betrayed.

Addressing the Brazilian Association for American Studies, Hollinger took pains to note that "the need to confront, rather than 'erase' conflicts 'of regions, race, class, gender, and sexual-ity' has long been accepted in a variety of academic settings in the United States and was a well-established mantra against the 'con-sensus' school even in the 1970s." He went on to say that "if some-one is looking for ways to innovate in American Studies, or if one wants to develop a perspective influenced by one's position as an outsider to the United States, the place to look is not the differ-ences by region, race, class, gender, and sexuality."[7] He was trying to warn his Brazilian audience against repeating a familiar mantra under the illusion that they were boldly breaking new paths.

Hollinger's speech in Brazil runs counter to a warning ut-tered by Janice Radway in her 1998 Presidential Address. There

she said that the American Studies Association must "ensure
that its very name does not enforce the achievement of premature closure through an implicit, tacit search for the distinc-
tively American 'common ground.'" What Hollinger views as
ceasing to repeat a mantra is viewed by Radway as "premature
closure." Radway continues by noting that in her address she
will not use the pronoun we, in the sense of "we Americans,"
because she wishes to refuse "the presumptive and coercive en-
closure it usually enacts when used in institutional situations of
this kind." "I have resisted," she continues, "the comforting assumption that there is an unproblematic 'we' as a way of recognizing that the many who associate their work with American studies
often have distinctly different interests, agendas, and concerns."[8]

Radway may here be making implicit reference to a well-
known paper by Hollinger titled "Expanding the Circle of the
'We.'" There Hollinger treats the process of taking account of
the needs and concerns of blacks, women, gays, lesbians, and
recent immigrants to the United States as attempts to make
phrases like "We, the people of the United States" or "we fellow-
citizens" cover more kinds of people than they had in the past.
He sees the search for greater social justice as the attempt to
change "them" into "us," to include the concerns of the previously excluded in deliberation about what, politically, is to be
done. He views the various movements toward including the
excluded as not so much recognition of difference—cultural or
otherwise—but of incorporation in a larger unity.

This strikes people like Singh and Radway as condescend-
ing—as a perpetuation of the attitude that says, "You people
down at the bottom should be patient until we wise and good
middle-class white males have the time to raise you up to equal
status with ourselves and then to assimilate you." This sort of
condescension was, they point out, the customary attitude of

men toward women who asked for the right to vote, of Southern whites toward African-Americans who asked not to be lynched, and of Northern whites toward blacks who asked to be hired on the same terms as their white competitors. Practitioners of "cultural studies" such as Singh and Radway want the various disadvantaged and oppressed groups within US society who have been subjected to such lofty condescension to resist and want each of them to retain a kind of proud autonomy rather than simply hoping to be assimilated into the larger society. This is why they distrust Hollinger's proposal to stop practicing identity politics and why they refuse to switch from criticism of American culture to criticism of the American government.

From Hollinger's and my point of view, this justified suspicion of condescension goes too far when it expresses itself as suspicion of any attempt to get a consensus among Americans—any attempt to unite Americans behind ideals which, though dishonored in the past, have some chance of being honored in the future. We are particularly dubious about Radway's argument that "the state and the political economy of the United States are themselves entirely dependent on the internal, imperial racialization of the population" and that the United States "is thus utterly dependent on its obsession with 'blackness'... that obsession is constitutive of the state." "Entirely" and "utterly" seem to us rhetorical overstatements, essentialistic oversimplifications, ways of avoiding asking how things might be changed.

Liberals like Hollinger and myself are dubious about identity politics because we think that it is merely mystificatory to run together a community of interest with an "identity" or with "a shared culture." We see the black poor and the white poor in the United States as having a shared interest, and we regard the question of whether they share a common culture as politically irrelevant. From the point of view of our radical opponents,

however, this distaste for identity politics is a result of our failure to realize how deeply the black-white contrast permeates
our culture. Our insistence on thinking in terms of competing,
and possibly cooperating, interest groups rather than in terms
of cultural differences signalizes our failure to realize that the
difference between African-Americans and Americans of other
ethnic backgrounds is not much like that between, for example,
Irish Americans and WASP Americans, or between Jewish
Americans and Arab Americans. In particular, we fail to grasp
the implications of the fact that the conviction that "one drop of
black blood pollutes" is not matched by any similar conviction in
regard to Irish or Jewish or Vietnamese or Hispanic blood.

We liberals respond to this line of criticism by saying that the
United States has always been a multicultural society, one that
in the past has often been united by a sense of shared citizenship
and of shared hope for political change. We think it essential to
keep both of these alive. We have to concede to the radicals that
for African-Americans, and for the Japanese Americans who
were interned after Pearl Harbor, the promise of equal citizenship was not fulfilled. We also have to concede that the belief
that "one drop of black blood pollutes" means that intermarriage will probably not break down barriers for African-
Americans in the way it did for immigrant groups in the past
(and probably will for Hispanic and Asian-Americans). But we
think it important to reemphasize that the promise of equal
citizenship was fulfilled, eventually, in respect to the immigrants who arrived from Europe between 1850 and 1920. Insofar
as "multiculturalism" simply means "antiracism," then liberals
can be as good multiculturalists as can radicals. But the radicals
seem not to think that "antiracism" is an adequate synonym. We
liberals cannot see what more "multiculturalism" could mean.

The disagreements between liberal and radical scholars in the United States about the nature of our country are mirrored by their respective ways of looking at the Bush administration's overweening arrogance since 9/11—its assumption that US hegemony should go unquestioned and that the other nations should be content to have the United States police the world.

From the point of view of the radicals—people whose view of the United States is taken from the writings of Noam Chomsky and Gore Vidal—this arrogance is a matter of our having finally stripped off a mask, thus making the true nature of the United States becoming obvious to all. From the point of view of liberals like myself, however, it is a result of our having elected a particularly bad president in 2000. The radicals say, "America has finally unmasked itself, revealed itself as an unashamed imperial power." The liberals say, "Of course the people around Bush would like us to exercise unquestioned imperial hegemony, since that will increase American corporate profits, but their current dominance does not entail that they will always get their way." The difference is analogous to that between those who say, "Germany revealed its true nature when the Nazis took over," and those who say, "Germany had catastrophically bad luck in 1933 but proved able to overcome its own misfortune."

Liberals like myself are quite willing to drop the triumphalist Parringtonian paradigm, but we do not want to substitute a debunking, pessimistic account of the true nature of our country. As good pragmatists, we think that our country has a history, but not a nature. That history can be narrated in many different ways, but these narratives cannot be graded according to how close they come to an account of what our country really has been. None of them give us knowledge of an underlying national nature.

Those who, like myself, compose narratives in which our country figures as a symbol of the triumph of leftist ideals hope that the United States will have the power to act so as to realize and spread those ideals. There is a perfectly good leftist case for using the military power of democratic countries to conquer countries ruled by tyrants and to replace them with democratic regimes. That this excuse for invasion has been used disingenuously by, among others, Napoleon, Mussolini, Stalin, Mao, Eisenhower, Nixon, and Bush does not mean that it has to be used that way. To be leftist is to be internationalist, and to be internationalist is to believe that when a man such as Kim Il Song, Saddam Hussein, Pinochet, Milosevic, or Mugabe is victimizing the people of his country or of a neighboring territory, the peoples of the rest of the world should try to overthrow him.

The question of which country or international organization should do this, and whether it is to be done by invasion, assassination, or support of internal dissidence is a matter of calculating consequences, not one that can be settled by appeals to principle. Until the United Nations is transformed into what Tennyson called "the Parliament of Man," it will be up to individual democratic nation-states and coalitions of such states to overthrow tyrants. Recently, this has meant that it has been up to the United States. Sooner or later the European Union may pull itself together, increase its military budget, adopt a foreign policy of its own, and stride forth onto the world stage. But until that happens, the United States is the only nation likely to use its military power to right wrongs

In the present situation—one in which *pax Americana* is the best we can reasonably hope for—the American left should not try to make things easier for itself by adopting isolationism as a counterweight to oppose Bush's hypocritical interventionism. It should not worry about whether the United States is *really* a republic or *really* an empire, since it is obviously both. It should stick to the question of how we are going to use our imperial power—a question that is, precisely because we still are a republic, a matter for public debate.

As many commentators have been saying recently, the period of American imperial power is bound to be short-lived. We may be in the last decade of the *pax Americana*. People in the Bush administration seem honestly to believe that we can maintain our overwhelming military superiority forever; the "National Security Policy of the United States" makes this belief explicit. But nobody outside Washington takes seriously the idea that both China and Russia will be content to sit back and let the United States run the world for more than another few years. It is quite likely that the next time the United States embarks on an adventure abroad, its European allies, including Great Britain, will simply turn their backs on America and start sounding out the leaders of Russia and China about the possibility of forming a new peacekeeping coalition.

Still, with a great deal of prudence on America's part, plus a great deal of luck, the decline of American imperial power might see a transition to something better than the *pax Americana*—to a recognition by all the nuclear powers, including China and Russia, that they must work together to prevent an otherwise inevitable series of conflagrations. Whether America will have the necessary foresight and exercise the necessary prudence to make this transition possible will be determined, not by anything intrinsic to its nature or made inevitable by its history, but rather by a few million swing voters during the next three or four national elections. That is one of the splendors, as well as one of the miseries, of a republic.

15

POST-DEMOCRACY

ANTI-TERRORISM AND THE
NATIONAL SECURITY STATE
(2004)

Europe is coming to grips with the fact that al-Qaida's opponent is the West, not just the United States. The interior ministers of the European Union nations have been holding meetings to coordinate antiterrorist measures. The outcome of these meetings is likely to determine how many of their civil liberties Europeans will have to sacrifice.

We can be grateful that the 2004 attack in Madrid involved only conventional explosives. Within a year or two, suitcase-sized nuclear weapons (crafted in Pakistan or North Korea) may be commercially available. Eager customers will include not only rich playboys like Osama bin Laden but also the leaders of various irredentist movements that have metamorphosed into well-financed criminal gangs. Once such weapons are used in Europe, whatever measures the interior ministers have previously agreed to propose will seem inadequate. They will hold another meeting, at which they will agree on more draconian measures.

If terrorists do get their hands on nuclear weapons, the most momentous result will not be the death of hundreds of thousands of innocent people. It will be the fact that all the democracies will have to place themselves on a permanent war footing. The measures their governments will consider it necessary to impose are likely to bring about the end of many of the sociopolitical institutions that emerged in Europe and North America in the two centuries since the bourgeois revolutions. They may return the West to something like feudalism.

The actions of the Bush administration since September 11 have caused many Americans to think of the war on terrorism as potentially more dangerous than terrorism itself, even if it entailed nuclear explosions in many Western cities. If the direct effects of terrorism were all we had to worry about, their thinking goes, there would be no reason to fear that democratic institutions would not survive. After all, equivalent amounts of death and destruction caused by natural disasters would not threaten those institutions. If there were a sudden shift of tectonic plates that caused skyscrapers to collapse all around the Pacific Rim, hundreds of thousands of people would die within minutes. But the emergency powers claimed by governments would be temporary and local.

Yet if much less severe damage occurred as a result of terrorism, the officials charged with national security, those who bear the responsibility for preventing further attacks, will probably think it necessary to end the rule of law, as well as the responsiveness of governments to public opinion. Politicians and bureaucrats will strive to outdo one another in proposing outrageous measures. The rage felt when immense suffering is caused by human agency rather than by forces of nature will probably lead the public to accept these measures.

The result would not be a fascist putsch, but rather a cascade of governmental actions that would, in the course of a few years, bring about a fundamental change in the conditions of social life in the West. The courts would be brushed aside, and the judiciary would lose its independence. Regional military commanders would be given the kind of authority that once belonged to locally elected officials. The media would be coerced into leaving protests against government decisions unreported.

Fear of such developments is, of course, more common among Americans like me than among Europeans. For it is only in the US that the government has proclaimed a permanent state of war, and had that claim taken seriously by the citizens. Christopher Hitchens has jeeringly said that many American leftists are more afraid of John Ashcroft than they are of Osama bin Laden. I am exactly the sort of person Hitchens has in mind. Ever since the White House rammed the USA Patriot Act through Congress, I have spent more time worrying about what my government will do than about what the terrorists will do.

Questions about the constitutionality of the powers now being claimed by the executive branch have been endlessly debated in American law schools over the last two years. Some of these questions will come before the Supreme Court in April [2004—Eds.]. Two hundred and fifty towns and cities in the US have passed resolutions against the Patriot Act. Some of these resolutions direct local police forces not to cooperate with the federal government in enforcing the act's provisions. Those who framed and passed them see the act as a foretaste of much more extensive claims to emergency power that will be made once the terrorists mount a few more attacks within the United States on the scale of September 11.

The Patriot Act was a very complex *omnium gatherum*, hundreds of pages long. Like its British analogue, the Anti-Terrorism,

Crime and Security Act, it was rushed through in the wake of September 11. Both pieces of legislation were probably drawn up simply by asking the security agencies to list the restrictions they found most inconvenient. It is unlikely that a majority of members of Congress or of Parliament who voted for them had a clear idea of what they contained. We shall soon learn whether the Madrid bombings trigger the same sort of reaction by all or most of the governments of the EU.

Though I regard John Ashcroft as a thoroughly sinister figure, I don't think the Bush administration is filled with power-hungry crypto-fascists. Neither is the German or Spanish or British government. But I do think the end of the rule of law could come about almost inadvertently, in both the US and Europe, through the sheer momentum of the institutional changes that are likely to be made in the name of the war on terrorism. If there were a dozen successful terrorist attacks on European capitals, and if some of them used nuclear, biological, or chemical weapons, the military and the national security bureaucracies in all the European countries would, almost inevitably, be granted powers that they had not previously wielded. The public will find this fitting and proper. Local police forces will probably start working on instructions from the national capital. Any criticism by the media will be seen by the government as a source of aid and comfort to terrorism. European ministers of justice will echo Ashcroft's reply to critics of the Patriot Act. "To those who scare peace-loving people with phantoms of lost liberty," Ashcroft said, "my message is this: your tactics only aid terrorists, for they erode our national unity and diminish our resolve."

Such developments would gradually reduce the effectiveness of the various institutions that have made it possible for public opinion to influence the actions of democratic governments. At the end of this process of erosion, democracy would have been replaced by something quite different. This would probably be neither military dictatorship nor Orwellian totalitarianism, but rather a relatively benevolent despotism, imposed by what would gradually become a hereditary nomenklatura.

That sort of power structure survived the end of the Soviet Union and is now resolidifying under Putin and his fellow KGB alumni. The same structure seems to be taking shape in China and in Southeast Asia. In countries run in this way, public opinion does not greatly matter. Elections may still be held, but opposition parties are not allowed to pose any serious threat to the powers that be. Careers are less open to talent, and more dependent on connections with powerful persons. Since the courts and the police review boards are relatively powerless, it is often necessary for shopkeepers to pay protection money to the police, or to criminals tolerated by the police, in order to stay in business. It is dangerous for citizens to complain about corruption or about abuse of power by public officials. High culture is restricted to areas that are irrelevant to politics (as it was in the Soviet Union, and still is in China). No more uncensored media. No more student demonstrations. Not much in the way of civil society. In short, a return to something like the ancien régime, with the national security establishment of each country playing the role of the court at Versailles.

Life for much of the world would not be greatly changed if the dismal scenario I have just outlined were to play out in the West. For in the poor countries most of society has always been, and still is, organized along feudal lines. In northeast Brazil, as in the villages of equatorial Africa and Central Asia, nobody would notice that the world had changed, that a light had gone out. But in the countries in which the greatest moral progress has been made, that progress would cease. After a few generations, utopian fantasies of an open society might be cherished only by a few readers of old books.

Perhaps this prognosis is much too pessimistic. Maybe I, and the many Americans who share my fears, have been so frightened by Ashcroft that we have started to see monsters in every dark corner. Maybe European parliaments will not panic in the way that the US Congress did. Maybe democracy is more robust in European countries than in the US.

Still, I cannot help thinking that democratic institutions, in my country at least, have become pretty fragile. I am half (though only half) persuaded by the claim Chalmers Johnson makes in *The Sorrows of Empire* that "the United States is probably lost to militarism."[1] Johnson produces a lot of evidence to show that the "iron triangle" (the defense contractors, the Pentagon, and the armed services committees of Congress) has already acquired so much power that the best an American president can do is to negotiate with the Pentagon, rather than to give it orders. The military and the security agencies are not yet as powerful in the EU countries as they have become in the US, but they may suddenly see the chance, and the need, to seize powers they had not previously claimed—powers that will allow them to become the de facto rulers of their countries. Any such efforts would be cheered on by the military-industrial complex in Washington.

So much for the fears that I, and many others, have acquired since September 11, and that the Madrid bombings have reanimated. Is there anything the citizens of the Western democracies can do to make it less likely that their grandchildren will live under the sort of neofeudalism I have described? The only thing I can think of that might make a difference is a willingness to challenge the culture of government secrecy. Demands for government openness should start in the areas of nuclear weaponry and of intelligence-gathering—the places where the post–World War II obsession with secrecy began. As a first step, the citizenry could demand that their governments publish the facts about their stockpiles of weapons of mass destruction. Then they might insist that these governments make public the details of two sets of planned responses: one to the use of such weapons by other governments, and another for their use by criminal gangs such as al-Qaida.

They could also demand that their governments join in efforts to update the laws of war, and to create something like a code of international criminal justice. As many legal scholars have been pointing out since September 11, the laws of war were designed to cover the acts of national governments. Criminal law was intended to deal with acts committed within a nation's borders by its own citizens. There are plenty of grey areas where neither sort of law applies. In these areas, governments are now pretty much free to do as they please: to parachute hit squads into Third World countries in which terrorists are thought to be holding meetings, to bring about regime change in nations suspected of supporting terrorists, and so on. There is not much point in saying that such actions are against international law: they may prove to be the only way of preventing, for example, nerve gas in the London Underground, anthrax in the Bundestag, and a "dirty" nuclear device under the Seine next to Notre Dame. Updated laws, openly agreed on by international bodies and adopted, after debate, by national governments, would specify when such actions were legitimate. Such updating would provide a good occasion to draw up new multilateral agreements, and to think about using the United Nations for new purposes.

If Western governments were made to disclose and discuss what they plan to do in various sorts of emergency, it would at least be slightly harder for demagogic leaders to argue that the most recent attack justifies them in doing whatever they like. Crises are less likely to produce institutional change, and to have unpredictable results, if they have been foreseen and publicly discussed.

Open discussion of needed changes in international law should be accompanied by a new openness about many other topics. There is no good reason why the governments of France, Britain, the US, and Israel should not inform their citizens of the numbers and kinds of nuclear devices they have in stock, how much the weapons cost, how many of what kind they propose to build in future, and under what circumstances it is imagined that these devices would be used. Nor is there any reason not to disclose the full history of the development of chemical and biological weapons: to tell the American public, for example, why its tax money was used to develop something called "weapons-grade anthrax." And there is no reason to keep secret the budget and the functions of the US National Security Agency, or of its British equivalent at Cheltenham. It is time for the public to be shown the texts of the agreements between governments that have made it possible to girdle the globe with more than seven hundred US military bases. There was little enough reason for refusing to make this sort of information public even when the Cold War was at its height. It is hard to imagine what help its disclosure could give to the terrorists.

The progress humanity made in the nineteenth and twentieth centuries was largely due to the increased role of public opinion in determining government policies. But the lack of public concern about government secrecy has, in the last sixty years, created a new political culture in each of the democracies. In the US and in many of the EU countries, an elite has come to believe that it cannot carry out its mission of providing national security if its preparations are carried out in public. The events of September 11 greatly strengthened this conviction. Further attacks are likely to persuade those elites that they must destroy democracy in order to save it.

In a worst-case scenario, historians will someday have to explain why the golden age of Western democracy, like the age of the Antonines, lasted only about two hundred years. The saddest pages in their books are likely to be those in which they describe how the citizens of the democracies, by their craven acquiescence in governmental secrecy, helped bring the disaster on themselves.

16

HUMILIATION OR SOLIDARITY?

THE HOPE FOR A COMMON EUROPEAN
FOREIGN POLICY
(2003)

President Bush's national security adviser has said, according to newspaper reports, that Russia will be forgiven, Germany ignored, and France punished. Whether or not Condoleezza Rice actually used those words, they express the attitude of the Bush administration toward nations that failed to join the Iraq War

This article was written in response to a statement, authored by Jürgen Habermas and co-signed by Jacques Derrida, published in *Frankfurter Allgemeine Zeitung* on May 31, 2003. It called upon the nations of "Kerneuropa" (Donald Rumsfeld's "Old Europe"— France, Germany, Italy, Spain, Benelux, and Portugal) to adopt a common foreign policy. The Habermas-Derrida article was called "February 15th, or What Binds Europeans Together"—a reference to the day in 2003 on which mass demonstrations against the Iraq War were held in London, Rome, Madrid, Barcelona, Berlin, and Paris. It was also the day on which, in Habermas's words "the newspapers reported to their astonished readers the Spanish prime minister's invitation to the other European nations willing to support the Iraq war to swear an oath of loyalty to George W. Bush, an invitation issued behind the back of the other countries of the European Union." Other European philosophers (Umberto Eco, Adolf Muschg, Fernando Savater, and Gianni Vattimo) published statements along the same lines in the leading newspapers of their respective countries, also on May 31. The text below, representing an American reaction to the Habermas-Derrida initiative, was published in German in *Sueddeutsche Zeitung* on May 31. The Habermas-Derrida article was published in English in the September 2003 issue of *Constellations*.

coalition. Disagreement with Washington by foreign governments is being treated by the Bush White House not as honest difference of opinion but as the failure of knaves and fools to accept guidance from the wise, farsighted, and benevolent.

Rice herself (the former provost of my university) is a very sophisticated and knowledgeable scholar, and so it is unlikely that she thinks of European leaders in any such simplistic way. But her insistence on the need for America to retain total control of global affairs is consonant with the remark that the American press is now attributing to her. Presumably she thinks that people such as Joschka Fischer and Dominique de Villepin, though neither fools nor knaves, must nevertheless be publicly humiliated, in order to help ensure a stable world order. For such stability, on her view, will be possible only if America's hegemony goes unchallenged.

More frightening than the bullying tone adopted by President Bush's advisers is the fact that European heads of government and foreign ministers are now reverting to their bad old habits. They are competing with one another for Washington's favor. After so many decades of dependence, it is very hard for Europe's leaders to stop judging their success in foreign affairs by the extent to which they are on cordial terms with the great imperial power. But just insofar as they continue to do this, it will be easy for Washington to set them against one another— to make them behave like schoolchildren vying for the teacher's favor.

Jürgen Habermas and Jacques Derrida argue that "Europe must, within the framework of the United Nations, throw its weight on the scale in order to counterbalance the hegemonic unilateralism of the United States." If the statesmen of "Kerneuropa" adopt the stance that Habermas and Derrida recommend and act in concert to assert their independence of Washington, the US government will do everything possible to turn American public opinion against them. Refusal to accept the American magisterium will be viewed by most of the American media as a sign of moral weakness. Washington will also do its best to set the members of the European Union against one another, in order to ensure that Kerneuropa's audacity does not become an example for the EU as a whole. For the last thing Washington wants is a Europe that is sufficiently united and self-confident to question America's hegemony. If the citizens and governments of Kerneuropa act as Habermas and Derrida hope they will, Washington will use every trick in the book to get them back in line—to make sure that their countries' votes in the United Nations are determined by decisions made by Rice and her colleagues on the National Security Council. For Bush's advisers suspect that if the EU had held together—if its member governments had been unanimous and vociferous in their repudiation of Bush's adventurism—they would never have been able to persuade the American public to agree to the war in Iraq.

If the citizenry and the governments of Europe do not seize the hour, if they do not carry through on the repudiation of American unilateralism manifested on February 15, Europe is unlikely ever again to play a significant role in determining the future of the world. The leaders of France, Germany, Benelux, Italy, Portugal, and Spain cannot postpone the choice they have to make: whether to accept the humiliating subservience that Washington hopes to impose on them or to break free by formulating and pursuing foreign policy initiatives to which Washington will react with incredulous outrage.

For Americans who were horrified by the willingness of their fellow citizens (and of the Democratic Party) to support Bush's Iraq War, the acquiescence of European statesmen in American unilateralism would be a tragedy. For if Washington does force Germany to beg not to be ignored and France to plead for relief from punishment, then the next time an American president decides to embark on an exciting military adventure there will be no significant countervailing pressure from abroad. Remembering what happened the last time that Washington's will was defied, European governments will be loath to instruct their representatives at the UN to question the latest American initiative.

The Bush administration's view that a permanent *pax Americana*, one whose terms are dictated by Washington alone, is the world's only hope has as a corollary that the United States must never permit its military power to be challenged. That claim is made explicit in a policy statement titled "The National Security Strategy of the United States," which asserts, "Our forces will be strong enough to dissuade potential adversaries from pursuing a military build-up in hopes of surpassing, or equaling, the power of the United States."

It is possible that even Democratic presidents will, in the future, reiterate this claim to permanent hegemony. The bullying tone adopted by the Bush administration may be one that all future American presidential candidates feel compelled to adopt in order to show themselves "strong" and "resolute" in "making war against terrorism" (an expression that will be invoked, as David Bromwich has pointed out in these pages, to excuse anything the American government may choose to do).

This may be the case even though men like John Kerry, Howard Dean, and Richard Gephardt (the most plausible candidates for the Democratic presidential nomination next year) understand, as President Bush does not, that no empire lasts forever. They are farsighted enough to know that American economic and military dominance is bound to be transitory, and to suspect that insistence on perpetual military supremacy will, sooner or later, produce a confrontation with China, Russia, or both—a confrontation that may end in nuclear war. But this knowledge may not suffice to make them change the direction of American foreign policy.

This means that the European Union is the only likely sponsor of an alternative to Washington's project of a permanent *pax Americana*. The leaders of the still-fragile regimes that govern Russia and China are too preoccupied with their own hold on power, and with domestic problems, to ask themselves questions about the best course for the world as a whole. Their resentment at Washington's arrogance will remain tacit. They can afford to wait for their own day to come—the day on which they tell Washington that they can and will challenge its military power. If America refuses to recognize that that day will come sooner or later, and if Europe does nothing to offer an alternative scheme for world order, then nothing is likely to change. Sooner or later we shall recreate the situation that prevailed during the Cold War—nuclear powers daring each other to be the first to launch their missiles.

The rulers of at least a dozen countries will soon have their fingers on nuclear triggers. To believe that Washington can forever hold all these rulers in awe would be folly, yet it is a folly that seems likely to prevail. "The National Security Strategy of the United States" makes no reference to eventual nuclear disarmament, only to nonproliferation, where "nonproliferation" means that only regimes that acknowledge American hegemony have the right to possess nuclear weapons. That document pretends that the danger of nuclear confrontation ended when the Cold War ended and takes for granted that American and Russian submarines, each of them armed with enough warheads to destroy ten great cities, will lurk beneath the oceans for generations to come.

Prior to the Bush administration, American statesmen usually paid lip service, at least, to the idea that the *pax Americana* was a transition to something better. Most of them realized that American hegemony was a makeshift that would have to do until something more enduring became possible—something like a veto-free United Nations functioning as a global parliament, equipped with a permanent peacekeeping military force and able to carry out a program of global disarmament. (I once heard a former Republican secretary of state say, in private, that he would be willing to trade a considerable measure of American national sovereignty for nuclear disarmament.) For Bush and his advisers, talk of such a rebuilt UN is pointlessly idealistic, a refusal to face up to reality, a romantic retreat into a dream world.

If any projects for a new international order put forward by the EU are to be of use, they will have to embody the idealism that America has seemingly become unable to sustain. The EU will have to put forward a vision of the world's future to which Washington will react with scornful mockery. It will have to offer proposals for rewriting the Charter of the United Nations and for putting the UN in charge of a program of global nuclear disarmament. It will have to dream dreams that will strike Realpolitikers as absurd. But, as Habermas and Derrida point out, some of Europe's recent dreams have come true. They are right to say that Europe has, in the second half of the twentieth century, found a solution to the problem of how to transcend the nation-state. The EU—just as it stands, even prior to the adoption of a constitution—is already the realization of what the Realpolitikers thought was an idle fantasy. If the sense of shared European citizenship becomes entrenched in the first quarter of the twenty-first century in the way in which the sense of shared American citizenship became entrenched in the last quarter of the eighteenth century, the world will be well on the way to a global confederation. Such a confederation has been recognized, ever since Hiroshima, as the only long-term solution to the problem created by nuclear weapons.

"Why," Habermas and Derrida ask, "should not Europe . . . devote itself to the broader goal of defending a cosmopolitan world-order based on international law against competing initiatives?" Why not indeed? If Europe did that, it might just save the world, something that American policy cannot do. At best, America's "national security strategy" can only postpone disaster. It can only keep things going for another generation or two. If there is ever a time when public opinion must force politicians to be more idealistic than they feel comfortable being, this is it. For all the reasons Habermas and Derrida give, the citizens of Kerneuropa are in the best position to exert such pressure.

If February 15, 2003, comes to be seen, as Habermas and Derrida hope it may, as the "birth of a European public sphere," the beginning of a new sense of shared European identity, that would change everyone's sense of what is politically possible. Such an upsurge of idealistic self-redefinition would be responded to around the world, in the United States and China as well as in Brazil and Russia. It would break the logjam that we are now trapped in. It is, as far as I can see, about the only thing that might.

Bush's apologists in the American media are likely to dismiss such initiatives as Habermas's and Derrida's as just further examples of the envious and resentful anti-Americanism that is recurrent among European intellectuals. Such a charge would be completely baseless. Both philosophers have profited from their frequent and extended visits to the United States to gain a deep and thorough understanding of America's political and cultural achievements. They are well aware of America's world-historical role as the first of the great constitutional democracies, and also of what America has done for Europe in the years since World War II. They appreciate that it was idealistic Wilsonian internationalism in the United States that led to the creation of the United Nations. They know that the unilateralist arrogance of the Bush administration is a contingent misfortune—neither inevitable nor expressive of something deeply embedded, and irredeemable, in American culture and society.

Both Europe and America contain many millions of people who see clearly that, despite all that America has done for the cause of human freedom, its assertion of a right to permanent hegemony is a terrible mistake. Americans who realize this need all the help they can get to persuade their fellow citizens that Bush has been taking their country down the wrong path. The solidification of the European Union into a powerful independent force in world affairs would be viewed by that segment of American opinion not as an expression of resentful anti-Americanism but as an entirely appropriate and altogether welcome reaction to the danger that the direction of American foreign policy poses for the world.

17

HALF A MILLION BLUE HELMETS?

(1995)

Visiting Belgrade last year, I asked my hosts, the antiwar intellectuals of the Belgrade Circle, what the United States might do to help with the situation in Bosnia.[1] They replied that there is no big geopolitical problem to be resolved, but simply a lot of very well armed gangs led by very cruel warlords. Each gang is in business for itself, and has a ready supply of cheap, ultramodern weapons at its disposal. Each forms fragile and temporary alliances with other gangs, as needed. None has any higher aims than loot and rape for the private soldiers, and Swiss bank accounts for the warlords themselves. Ethnicity and ideology are pretty much beside the point, except for initial recruitment purposes.

On the account offered by my Serbian hosts, what was needed was neither diplomatic negotiation nor sage reflection on the history of the Balkans, but a lot of very heavily armed policemen. For the situation on the borders of Bosnia is not much different from the situation in parts of Los Angeles or Chicago. Lots of decent people in the middle of ex-Yugoslavia, who did not want to hurt their neighbors, have been forced to do so by gangs of thugs—just as have lots of similar people in the middle of Chicago, the people who have found it impossible to get protection from the city's police. These citizens of Chicago pay taxes to a government that gives them few services in return, largely because the city's budget is starved of the money that the surrounding suburbs lavish on themselves. The people in Bosnia pay tribute to warlords rather than taxes to governments, largely because the United Nations' budget is starved of money which is spent by the industrial democracies on themselves.

Much of the money we in the industrial democracies spend on ourselves is earned by making and selling cluster bombs, white phosphorus, machine pistols, ground-to-air missiles, and other items that make it easier for warlords in places like Burundi and Bosnia to keep control of the people they have terrorized. Getting the money we in the American suburbs use to ensure our comfort and security requires keeping a vast reserve army of the unemployed in the inner cities, thereby ensuring that no more than a miserable minimum wage need be paid for any unskilled job. We spend a lot of time deploring the violent habits of people who, unlike ourselves, are unable to rely on a state's monopoly of force for their protection. But we profit greatly from the conditions that make this violence inevitable.

Still, even if we in the comfortable suburbs of Chicago and Los Angeles remain unwilling to pay decent wages for the services required from our fellow citizens, we might conceivably be persuaded to pay for the services of policemen to keep the gangs in foreign countries under control. We are not yet quite so selfish as to be indifferent to the genocide in Bosnia and Rwanda. We keep saying that we should like to do something. We may be too scared of losing our comfort and security to seriously consider sharing our wealth with the people who serve us hamburgers and mop our office floors, but we might not mind using some of the gigantic American defense budget to save a few foreign lives and homes.

Nevertheless, whenever this possibility comes up, we hear nothing from Washington except details of the insuperable difficulties presented by any concrete proposal for action. This makes us remember that no American president is any longer likely to risk reelection by giving orders that will result in American deaths, unless these deaths are incurred in the course of a quick and overwhelming victory. Such a victory is never possible when suppressing a *Bandenkrieg*.[2] Yet more and more *Bandenkriege* lie ahead for most of the poor countries (even for the largest ones, China and Russia, in which nuclear arms are lying around for the taking).

Fifty years ago, we thought that the world had learned its lesson from the failure of the League of Nations in Ethiopia, and that the United Nations would be different. Maybe it still could be. Rendered irrelevant by the Cold War for most of those fifty years, the UN now might get a new lease on life. Suppose that we just forgot about the now laughable idea of "American world leadership" and, more generally, about the idea that each individual industrial democracy must form an independent judgment about each new *Bandenkrieg*. Suppose the politicians of the industrialized democracies got together and agreed that their political lives are being unnecessarily complicated by the recurrent need to hide do-nothing foreign policies behind fiercely moralistic rhetoric. These politicians might agree that it would be worth giving the UN some real power, if doing so enabled them to avoid recurrent embarrassment.

Suppose, more concretely, that the industrialized democracies placed half of their crack units at the disposal of a UN-appointed general military staff. This would mean that half of

the Marine combat divisions, of the Army Rangers, of the Navy
SEALS, and of Tom Clancy's other favorite outfits (plus their
equivalents in the armed forces of Britain, France, Spain, Germany, India, Brazil, etc.) would be available for suppressing
Bandenkriege at the drop of a Security Council resolution. These
units are made up of the kind of young men (and, nowadays,
young women) who are not only able to contemplate risking
their lives in violent and completely unpredictable combat, but
who actually relish the thought of doing so. There will always
be a lot of young people of this sort, and it would be nice if their
energies and talents could be turned to a useful purpose. Such
people are as hard for most of us wimpy intellectuals to understand as we are for most of them. But like us, they have their uses.

Brave young people of this sort have always been eager to
join police and military forces. Not many of them are sadists
(even though a few of them always will be, just as will a few of
us intellectuals). They are, for the most part, decent people who
see much of the world as at the mercy of armed bad guys, and
who would like to do something about it. If they realized that
they might actually have a chance of fighting not in order to
preserve the comfort of the suburbs, or low petroleum prices,
but to save innocent people from ruthless thugs, they might
start signing up in their country's crack units with the explicit
hope of being assigned to UN service. Eventually the various
national armed forces might exchange a guarantee of such service
for a long-term reenlistment by a noncommissioned officer.

If these sorts of arrangements could be worked out, we
might, in a decade or two, have a full-fledged, experienced,
battle-hardened, international police force of, say, half a million
men and women. These people would be paid and armed by
their respective nations, but their esprit de corps would be
largely a result of being Blue Helmets, the men and women who

had come to the protection of innumerable widows and orphans, and had made return to their homes possible for countless miserable refugees.

The experienced general officers commanding these Blue Helmets would come to have the sort of influence on Security Council decisions, and on public opinion, that an honest and experienced police chief has on the decisions of his city's mayor and councilors. These officers would be able to fill the skies of a given area with the very latest planes, equipped with the very latest defense against ground-to-air missiles and the very latest pinpoint aiming devices. They could call on the navies of the world to carry them anywhere they needed to go.

The arms industry (a sector of the economy whose power can be deduced from the fact that so little about it ever hits the newspapers, or the TV screens) would make even greater profits. It could sell its latest products to governments for use by the Blue Helmets, while selling only slightly obsolete, or perhaps slightly defective, products to the warlords. It could thus do well by doing good.

It would be nice, of course, if we could put these cynical merchants of death out of business, just as it would be nice if we could do something about the cocaine and heroin industries, and about the people in China and Russia who are busy converting their countries' publicly owned productive capacities into privately owned Swiss francs. But nobody seems to know what is to be done about these various problems. By contrast, the *Bandenkriege*, and the endless horrors that they are producing, seem a soluble problem.

For not much would have to change to provide half a million Blue Helmets. No special interests would be greatly damaged. The various military-industrial complexes would survive intact. There would be protests from miscellaneous ethnic groups in the capitals of the industrialized democracies whenever the Security Council took action, but nobody would much care. The local politicians could escape blame by protesting that they would never dream of interfering with a UN decision. There would be the same consensus among the respectables about the need to go get the warlords as there is among the American middle class about the need to be tough on crime.

I shall be told that, in an America in which millions of people believe that the UN is about to take over the United States by deploying its secret fleet of black helicopters, this proposal is "politically impossible." I am not sure that, if we ever got a president who combined Clinton's intelligence and decency with Truman's guts, it would remain impossible. But suppose it is. There are a lot of other countries in the world. It would take no more than an agreement among half a dozen of the richest of them to give such a proposal a fighting chance.

America did the world a lot of good (and, of course, a lot of incidental harm) by defeating the fascists in World War II and the communists in the Cold War. But America now seems to be having a nervous breakdown: the country is exhausted, dispirited, frightened, irresolute, and utterly unable to contribute to the resolution of international problems. My country may recover some day. I hope it does. But the attempt to create a big international police force (a force whose creation has been urged many times in the past, by people who know a lot more than I do) need not wait on that distant event.

18

A QUEASY AGNOSTICISM

(2005)

Once they could no longer believe in the immortality of the soul, many Westerners substituted the project of improving human life on Earth for that of getting to Heaven. Hoping for the achievement of Enlightenment ideals took the place of yearning to see the face of God. Spiritual life came to center around movements for social change, rather than around prayer or ritual.

Most of those who made that switch took for granted that the West would retain its hegemony long enough to bring liberty, equality, and fraternity to the rest of the planet. But that hegemony is over. The West has reached its acme; it is as rich and powerful as it is going to get. Even the United States of America can deploy military power only by risking bankruptcy. The American Century has ended, and the Chinese Century has begun. America, while in the saddle, did more good than harm. Nobody knows what China will do—least of all the Chinese.

Yet economic and military decline is not the only problem for the West. It may be frightened into renouncing its ideals even before it loses its influence. Suppose a dirty nuclear bomb, hidden in the bowels of a container ship, were exploded in San

Francisco Bay. Could a free press and an independent judiciary survive martial law? Would Germany remain a constitutional democracy if such a bomb went off at the Hamburg docks? The first terrorists to containerize a stolen nuclear warhead may be able to preen themselves on having demolished institutions that took two centuries to build.

In the course of those centuries, Western idealists swung back and forth between exuberance and desperation. The first is captured by Alfred Tennyson in "Locksley Hall":

> Not in vain the distance beacons. Forward, forward let
>   us range,
> Let the great world spin forever down the ringing grooves
>   of change.
> Thro' the shadow of the globe we sweep into the
>   younger day;
> Better fifty years of Europe than a cycle of Cathay.

But when things go badly we reread Matthew Arnold's "Dover Beach":

> . . . we are here as on a darkling plain
> Swept with confused alarms of struggle and flight,
> Where ignorant armies clash by night.

In early 1914 it was still possible to be confident that, given another fifty years of Europe, the world would be transformed, and greatly improved. But as the twentieth century piled up its catastrophes, more and more writers told us it would be foolish to hope. "It is closing time in the gardens of the West," Cyril Connolly wrote just before the Second World War, "and from now on an artist will be judged only by the resonance of his solitude or the quality of his despair." But Connolly was wrong. The war turned out better than he had any reason to expect.

Even Auschwitz did not stop successive postwar generations from thinking that the world might still, under Western guidance, sweep forward into a younger day.

But the postwar impetus has faltered, and the attacks of September 11, 2001, have made us realize how unlikely it is that the West will be able to determine the world's future. It is dawning on non-Western nations that their fates will rest with Beijing rather than with Washington. How long Europeans and Americans have to stroll the gardens depends upon how long keeping them open remains in the interests of Cathay.

The tragedy of the modern West is that it exhausted its strength before being able to achieve its ideals. The spiritual life of secularist Westerners centered on hope for the realization of those ideals. As that hope diminishes, their life becomes smaller and meaner. Hope is restricted to little, private things—and is increasingly being replaced by fear.

This change is the topic of Ian McEwan's novel *Saturday*. One of the characters—Theo, the eighteen-year-old son of Henry Perowne, the middle-aged neurosurgeon who is the novel's protagonist—says to his father,

> When we go on about the big things, the political situation, global warming, world poverty, it all looks really terrible, with nothing getting better, nothing to look forward to. But when I think small, closer in—you know, a girl I've just met, or this song we are doing with Chas, or snowboarding next month, then it looks great. So this is going to be my motto— think small.

John Banville, who, in the *New York Review of Books*, finds the novel a distressing failure, says that this "might also be the motto of McEwan's book." But thinking small is not the novel's motto; it is its subject. McEwan is not urging us to think small.

He is reminding us that we are increasingly tempted to do so. Banville is off the mark yet again when he says that "the politics of the book is banal." The book does not have a politics. It is about our inability to have one—to sketch a credible agenda for large-scale change.

Saturday has an epigraph from Saul Bellow's *Herzog* that speaks of "the late failure of radical hopes." McEwan's long quotation from one of Moses Herzog's soliloquies ends, "The beautiful supermachinery opening a new life for innumerable mankind. Would you deny them the right to exist? Would you ask them to labor and go hungry while you yourself enjoyed old-fashioned Values? You—you yourself are a child of this mass and a brother to all the rest. Or else an ingrate, dilettante, idiot. There, Herzog, thought Herzog, since you ask for the instance, is the way it runs."

The problem for good-hearted Westerners like Henry Perowne is that they seem fated to live out their lives as idiots (in the old sense of "idiot," in which the term refers to a merely private person, one who has no part in public affairs). They are ingrates and dilettantes—ingrates because their affluence is made possible by the suffering of the poor and dilettantes because they are no longer able to relate thought to action. They cannot imagine how things could be made better.

But secular Western liberals would still like to think of themselves as brothers to all the rest. So when Henry encounters a man of his own age energetically sweeping the gutters near his home, he muses that "his vigor and thoroughness are uncomfortable to watch, a quiet indictment on a Saturday morning." But his only response to this indictment is to think,

How restful it must have been, in another age, to be prosperous and believe that an all-knowing supernatural force had

allotted people to their stations in life. And not to see how
the belief served your own prosperity. . . . Now we think we
do see, how do things stand? After the ruinous experiments
of the recently deceased century, after so much vile behavior,
so many deaths, a queasy agnosticism has settled around
these matters of justice and redistributed wealth. No more
big ideas. The world must improve, if at all, by tiny steps.
People mostly take an existential view—having to sweep the
streets for a living looks like simple bad luck. It's not a visionary age. The streets need to be clean. Let the unlucky enlist.

After the ruinous experiments, after the late failure of radical
hopes, it has become hard to find inspiration in a vision of a
just, free, global community. It remained a visionary age, and an
intense spiritual life remained possible for secularized Westerners, only as long as it seemed possible to take more than tiny
steps. Even if we have some middle-sized ideas about how to
make things better—narrowing the income gap between gray-
haired neurosurgeons and gray-haired gutter-sweepers, for
example—we have no plausible ideas about how to alleviate "the
political situation, global warming, world poverty."

Even if we got some new big ideas, it seems unlikely that we
would have time to implement them. For our cities are vulnerable. As the novel begins, Henry looks out his bedroom win-
dow and sees a jetliner in flames. It is flying along the Thames
and may perhaps swerve and hit the old Post Office Tower. If
the Tower falls, it will crush Henry and his family.

The plane turns out to be harmless, but later in the day Perowne thinks, "The government's counsel—that an attack in a
European or American city is an inevitability—isn't only a
disclaimer of responsibility, it's a heady promise. Everyone
fears it, but there's also a darker longing in the collective mind, a

sickening for self-punishment and a blasphemous curiosity." We sicken for self-punishment because of the guilt that comes from being able to do little and being unable to imagine doing more, either for gutter-sweepers in London or for children in Guatemalan sweatshops. We feel that our world does not deserve to last, because it is so irredeemably unjust.

Perowne's reflections are embedded within a plot that turns on a chance, and potentially fatal, encounter with a thug named Baxter. Baxter, as it happens, is in the early stages of a devastating disease—Huntington's Chorea. Perowne recognizes the symptoms. He avoids being beaten senseless by telling Baxter, falsely, that he may be able to provide a cure. Later in the day, however, a freshly enraged Baxter invades Perowne's home, accompanied by a subordinate thug. The two force Perowne's daughter to strip naked and hold a knife to his wife's throat. The talented, decent, generous Perowne family is in deadly danger.

Then, manifesting the quirky mood-switching whimsicality that is one of the symptoms of his disease, Baxter picks up the naked daughter's freshly published volume of poems from a table and orders her to recite one of them. Her grandfather, himself a distinguished poet, intervenes and tells her, in cryptic language, to recite "Dover Beach" instead. She does so, and, miraculously, it works. Baxter's mood switches again: he is overcome by the sheer beauty of Arnold's lines. Now he can once again be tricked into believing that Henry will help him find a cure.

Baxter's failure to get on with raping and murdering infuriates his knife-wielding henchman, who walks out in disgust. That makes it feasible for young Theo to tackle Baxter, overcome him, and send for the police. Order and peace return to the Perowne house, the front windows of which look out upon "the perfect square laid out by Robert Adam enclosing a perfect circle of garden—an eighteenth-century dream bathed and embraced by modernity, by street light from above, and from below by fiber-optic cables, and cool fresh water coursing down pipes, and sewage borne away in an instant of forgetting."

The jet plane in flames turned out to be harmless, and Baxter to be vulnerable. But such luck is unlikely to last. There will be other planes and other thugs. The world outside the West is full of both. Some non-Western thugs may be fobbed off with the beauty of an eighteenth-century dream, but hardly all. The mood of some may change, but others will stay the course. So, within Theo's lifetime, cool fresh water may cease to run beneath London. "The future," Perowne meditates, "will look back on us as gods, certainly in this city, lucky gods blessed by supermarket cornucopias, torrents of accessible information, warm clothes that weigh nothing, extended life-spans, wondrous machines." But not only affluence will vanish; so will hope.

At one point in the novel Perowne tries to overcome what he thinks of as "the source of his vague sense of shame or embarrassment—his readiness to be persuaded that the world has changed beyond recall, that harmless streets like this and the tolerant life they embody can be destroyed by the new enemy." He tries to convince himself that "the world has not fundamentally changed. Talk of a hundred-year crisis is an indulgence. There are always crises, and Islamic terrorism will settle into place, alongside recent wars, climate changes, the politics of international trade, land and fresh water shortages, hunger, poverty and the rest."

Maybe it will, or maybe 9/11 will prove to have been the harbinger of far more terrible events. Maybe the gardens will stay open for quite a while, or maybe they will close much sooner than we think. McEwan has no more certainty about these matters than do the rest of us. But his novel helps bring us up-to-date about ourselves. It makes vivid both our uneasiness about the future and our queasy, debilitating agnosticism about matters of justice and redistributed wealth.

AFTERWORD

The end of a chronological period—whether a century or a
millennium—invites speculation about the extent to which
progress has occurred during that period: Has humanity as a
whole become more grown up, less childish?

As soon as one tries to tell a story of the maturation of humanity as a whole, one realizes that the very idea of such a story
is relatively new. In Europe, at least, it is not much older than
the eighteenth century—the century that witnessed the framing of the first great European narrative of human self-fashioning
(Giambattista Vico's) as well as a growing conviction that
human beings might be entirely on their own in the world, bereft of guidance from above. Before that time, most people took
for granted that human life—with all the familiar violence and
cruelty that had always afflicted it—would never be very different from what it had always been, and that the fate of humanity
did not rest in human hands.

The eighteenth century also saw the French Revolution—the
event that created our modern political consciousness. The idea
that human beings could take charge of history and create an egalitarian utopia, a world without caste, class, or institutionalized

cruelty, gained credibility only after the cataclysm of 1789. The combination of an increasingly secular culture and of revolutionary political hope inspired the second great European epic of human maturation, Hegel's *Lectures on the Philosophy of History*. The eighteenth century in Europe is often referred to as the age of Enlightenment: the age when the Europeans broke the spell of religious superstition, ceased to hope that they would be compensated in Heaven for their suffering on earth, and realized that the only paradise they could strive for was a terrestrial one. Since the Enlightenment, stories of human maturation and of human decline have proliferated in Europe, and have usually been unself-consciously Eurocentric. Hegel and Marx have offered the most familiar Eurocentric narratives of maturation, and Nietzsche and Heidegger the most familiar Eurocentric narratives of decline.

The former narratives present themselves as stories of emancipation—of liberation from fetters, of an ascent from slavery to freedom. But "emancipation" is ambiguous. Sometimes it means freedom from hunger, toil, cruelty, and humiliation. In other contexts it means being released from subjugation to mistaken ideas, emerging from intellectual darkness into intellectual light—a process often described as "becoming more rational."

The philosophers who have written such stories tend to assume that human beings will treat each other decently—will cease to be cruel to one another exactly insofar as they replace appearance with reality, a corrupt religion with a pure religion, or a false philosophy with a true philosophy. The possibility of such a true philosophy, it is further supposed, was first glimpsed in Europe in the eighteenth century, the period when science usurped the place of religion at the center of high culture.

The ambiguity between these two meanings of "emancipation" has caused considerable confusion in recent decades, and the premise that the European eighteenth century saw both intellectual and political progress has been subjected to extensive criticism. Writers like Michel Foucault have suggested a new view of the European Enlightenment: for Foucault, the eighteenth century was an era in which the fetters that have always bound humanity were reforged rather than shattered. Intellectuals who think of themselves as "postmodern" often maintain that we have now seen through the myth of Enlightenment. Friedrich Nietzsche, Martin Heidegger, and Jacques Derrida are supposed to have shown us that the ideas of "Nature" and of "Reason" that dominated eighteenth-century European thought are mere illusions.

But whereas Nietzsche and Heidegger despised attempts to create an egalitarian utopia, many of the intellectuals who agree with them that the rationalism of the Enlightenment is philosophically indefensible—that we no longer have a use for the idea that a world without cruelty would be "more in accord with Nature" or "more rational" than a world ruled by the lash and the knout—nevertheless believe that the Enlightenment saw the beginnings of a movement toward human equality that is still worth fighting and dying for. Philosophers such as Derrida, for example, hold that "democracy" is still a near-synonym of the most precious human ideal: justice. Like the American pragmatist philosopher John Dewey, Derrida has no use for the rationalist tradition that binds Plato together with Kant; yet again like Dewey, his enthusiasm for a world without caste, class, or cruelty remains undiminished.

In the circumstances, I think it is best simply to admit that change in opinion among the intellectuals—a change from a religious to a secular culture, or from a rationalist to a postmodern philosophical view—may be largely irrelevant to the creation of the sort of society that Derrida, Dewey, and most of the rest of us dream about. A narrative of emancipation from cruelty, of the development of what the Israeli philosopher Avishai Margalit calls "a decent society," defined as one where social institutions do not humiliate, can be spun without much reference to religion or philosophy, to the views people hold about the existence or nonexistence of God, or about the nature of Truth or Reason. We should not presume that there is a tight connection between the attainment of decency in human relations and the ascendancy of a particular worldview.

Nor should we imagine that any single European intellectual tradition—or Asian or African one for that matter—is clearly more favorable to bringing about a decent society than any other. It may be that the difference between Confucianism and Christianity, or between scientific rationalism and postmodernism, is just froth on the surface compared to the difference between a society in which there are untouchable castes and one in which there are not, or between a society where some people have thousands of times as much money as others and one where income differences are relatively slight. It may be that a decent society can be constructed without paying a great deal of attention to either religion or philosophy.

If this is true, then speculation about the coming millennium and our chances of making further progress is not a matter for professors of philosophy like myself, but for economists, political analysts, and demographers. The story of human maturation toward an egalitarian, decent society should be separated from the question of whether one continent's intellectual tradition is more "advanced" than another's.

The idea of "advanced thought" can perhaps be set aside altogether. We would do well to abandon the notion that there is some final worldview to which the world's civilizations are destined to converge. A decent, even utopian global society could contain dozens of worldviews—some centering on religion, some on science, and still others on art. They might have nothing more in common than the conviction that humiliation and cruelty are terrible evils, evils that men and women of goodwill can join together and overcome.

The big question about the coming century, and about the coming millennium, is not what the intellectuals will be talking about when it ends, nor about which religions and philosophies will have survived, but whether the gradual diminution of the oppression of the weak by the strong that has marked the twentieth century will continue. For all the horrors of the past century, there is less systematic, institutionalized cruelty and humiliation at its close than at its beginning.

Imperialism of every sort—from that of Great Britain to that of the USSR, from straightforward military occupation to subtle economic domination—seems to be on the wane. Capitalism has in most countries been forced to partially decommodify labor; this has been accomplished by state intervention to set wages, hours, pensions, and working conditions.

Women are finally being allowed, in most of the world, to own property, get divorced, vote, and become educated. It is no longer permissible, in a steadily increasing number of societies, to humiliate people because of the color of their skin, or because of their ethnic or national origin. Decency has been on the rise for almost one hundred years. We have become more grown up: less like schoolyard bullies.

But economic and demographic pressures may quite possibly—and quite independently of any changes in religious or philosophical outlook—put the bullies back in control. With the ongoing globalization of the labor market, nobody knows whether the older industrialized democracies of Europe and North America, or the newly industrialized nations of Asia, will be able to hold on to the standard of living they currently enjoy. If that standard were to decline precipitately, wrenchingly, might not the survival of democratic institutions be imperiled? Nor can anyone really be sure that the so-called population bomb has not already exploded; despite a plethora of demographic forecasts and computer simulations, we still have no idea whether the planet can sustain the seven billion human beings who will shortly inhabit it. Conceivably some as yet unforeseen technological development will provoke ecological disaster; or some mad tyrant in Kazakhstan or North Korea or Zaire will decide to finance nuclear terrorism. Everything is, as the millennium comes, very fragile—far more fragile than it was in the eighteenth century. "Things," as Emerson said, "are in the saddle, and ride mankind."

We are constantly told that we can nevertheless save ourselves and continue the process of maturation, if only we undergo a "spiritual renewal." I suspect that this is whistling in the dark. What it will take to get us through the next century, and to make the next millennium one of continued progress toward a decent society, is practical ingenuity.

We shall have to be very clever to cope with the global economy, and with the magnificent opportunities for exploitation it affords the superrich and the kleptocratic tyrants. We shall have to be very innovative in our attempts to put a brake on population growth. We shall have to be very quick and resolute in dealing with nuclear and ecological threats.

Neither a new religion nor a new philosophy will be of much avail in any of this. What will help is a breed of leaders with sufficient imagination to propose bold yet concrete solutions—solutions to be debated by the newly literate populations of the world's democracies.

NOTES

Introduction: The Philosopher and His Country

1. Richard Rorty, *Achieving Our Country: Leftist Thought in Twentieth-Century America* (Cambridge, MA: Harvard University Press, 1998), 90, 88.

2. These and other biographical tidbits expressed in this paragraph come from Rorty's autobiographical essay, "Trotsky and the Wild Orchids," in *Philosophy and Social Hope* (New York: Penguin Books, 1999), 3–20. For an intellectual biography that covers his life and work up to 1982, see Neil Gross, *Richard Rorty: The Making of an American Philosopher* (Chicago: University of Chicago Press, 2008).

3. Rorty, *Philosophy and Social Hope*, 8.

4. Ibid., 6.

5. Ibid., 8.

6. See Richard Rorty, *Philosophy and the Mirror of Nature* (Princeton, NJ: Princeton University Press, 1979); and Rorty, "Philosophy as a Transitional Genre," in *The Rorty Reader*, ed. Christopher Voparil and Richard J. Bernstein (Malden, MA: Wiley-Blackwell, 2010), 473–88.

7. Richard Rorty, *Objectivity, Relativism, and Truth: Philosophical Papers, Vol. 1* (New York: Cambridge University Press, 1991), 178. For a full account of Rorty's philosophical development, see Christopher Voparil, "General Introduction," in Voparil and Bernstein, *Rorty Reader*, 1–52.

8. Richard Rorty, *Contingency, Irony, and Solidarity* (New York: Cambridge University Press, 1989), xvi.

9. Ibid., 176.

10. Gross, *Richard Rorty*, 97, 322.

11. Richard Rorty, "Pragmatism as Romantic Polytheism," in Voparil and Bernstein, *Rorty Reader*, 449.

12. Ibid., 450, 454.

13. Ibid., 447.

14. Richard Rorty, *Philosophy as Cultural Politics: Philosophical Papers, Vol. 4* (New York: Cambridge University Press, 2007), x. This stance echoes his call decades

earlier to revive the "celebrations of American democracy, naturalism, and social reconstruction" he associated with the "heroic period of Deweyan pragmatism," where philosophy provided "moral leadership" for the country. See Richard Rorty, *Consequences of Pragmatism* (Minneapolis: University of Minnesota Press, 1982), 61–64.

15. Rorty, *Achieving Our Country*, 36.

16. Richard Rorty, *Essays on Heidegger and Others: Philosophical Papers, Vol. 2* (New York: Cambridge University Press, 1991), 18; Rorty, *Contingency, Irony, and Solidarity*, 22.

17. Rorty, *Philosophy as Cultural Politics*, x.

18. Jonathan D. Culler, *Framing the Sign: Criticism and Its Institutions*, Oklahoma Project for Discourse and Theory 3 (Norman: University of Oklahoma Press, 1988), 55.

19. Dewey, qtd. on p. XX, this volume.

20. Posner, qtd. on p. XX, this volume.

21. Rorty, p. XX, this volume.

22. Rorty, p. XX, this volume.

23. Rorty, p. XX, this volume.

24. Rorty, p. XX, this volume.

25. Rorty, p. XX, this volume.

26. Rorty, p. XX, this volume.

27. Rorty, p. XX, this volume.

Chapter 1. Who Are We?

1. Richard A. Posner, "The Most Punitive Nation," *Times Literary Supplement*, September 1, 1995, 3.

Chapter 2. Democracy and Philosophy

1. Isaiah Berlin, *The Roots of Romanticism*, ed. Henry Hardy (Princeton, NJ: Princeton University Press, 1999), 23.

Chapter 3. Dewey and Posner on Pragmatism and Moral Progress

1. Leo Strauss, *Natural Right and History* (Chicago: University of Chicago Press, 1953), 6.

2. Kurt Gassen and Michael Landmann, eds., "Erinnerungen an Simmel von Rudolf Pannwit," in *Buch des Dankes an Georg Simmel: Briefe, Erinnerungen, Bibliographie* (Berlin: Duncker & Humboldt, 1958), 230, 240. ("Über den Pragmatismus sprach er [Simmel] einmal—in ein paar Sätzen—abschätzig: es wäre nur, was die Amerikaner sich aus Nietzsche geholt hätten.") I owe my knowledge of this passage to Wolf Lepenies.

3. Friedrich Nietzsche, *The Gay Science*, trans. Walter Kaufmann (New York: Vintage, 1974), sec. 354 at 300.

4. Ibid., sec. 344 at 283.

5. Friedrich Nietzsche, "The Will to Power: An Attempted Transvaluation of All Values," in *The Complete Works of Friedrich Nietzsche*, ed. Oscar Levy, trans. Anthony M. Ludovici (New York: Gordon, 1974), bk. III, sec. 481 at 12.

6. Nietzsche, *Gay Science*, sec. 373 at 335. ("Facts are precisely what is lacking, all that exists consists of *interpretations*. We cannot establish any fact 'in itself': it may even be nonsense to desire to do such a thing.")

7. Ibid., sec. 335 at 266.

8. John Dewey, "Philosophy and Democracy," in *John Dewey: The Middle Works, 1899–1924*, ed. Jo Ann Boydston (Carbondale: Southern Illinois University Press, 1982), 11:41, 45.

9. Ibid., 11:43.

10. John Dewey, "Moral Philosophy," in *John Dewey: The Early Works, 1882–1898*, ed. Jo Ann Boydston (Carbondale: Southern Illinois University Press, 1971), 4:147.

11. See Cheryl Misak, *Truth, Politics, Morality: Pragmatism and Deliberation* (New York: Routledge, 2000), 12–18 (noting that Dewey's view that philosophers should demonstrate humility coheres with an inclusive and egalitarian model of deliberative democracy); Robert Westbrook, *Democratic Hope: Pragmatism and the Politics of Truth* (Ithaca, NY: Cornell University Press, 2005), 187–88 (arguing that Dewey's democratic thought supports the establishment of a "community of inquiry," broadly characterized by debate, reason, and recognition, and one that is fully compatible with deliberative democracy).

12. Westbrook, *Democratic Hope*, 197.

13. Ibid., 200. ("For one might reasonably suppose that only the demand for more democracy will ensure that we do not get less democracy or even no democracy at all.")

14. Ibid., 189.

15. Richard A. Posner, *Law, Pragmatism, and Democracy* (Cambridge, MA: Harvard University Press, 2003), 113.

16. John Dewey, "The Public and Its Problems," in *John Dewey: The Later Works, 1925–1953*, ed. Jo Ann Boydston (Carbondale: Southern Illinois University Press, 1984), 2:235, 350.

17. Richard A. Posner, *The Problematics of Moral and Legal Theory* (Cambridge, MA: Belknap Press of Harvard University, 1999), 4.

18. Ibid.

19. Ibid., 6.

20. Ibid.

21. Ibid.

22. Ibid.

23. Ibid.

24. John Dewey, "Human Nature and Conduct," in *The Middle Works of John Dewey, 1899–1924*, ed. Jo Ann Boydston (Carbondale: Southern Illinois University Press, 1983), 14:164.

25. Posner, *Problematics of Moral and Legal Theory*, 30.

26. Ibid., 19–20.

27. Ibid., 19.

28. Ibid., 23.

29. Charles S. Peirce, "Some Consequences of Four Incapacities," in *Charles S. Peirce: Selected Writings*, ed. Philip P. Wiener (New York: Dover Publications, 1958), 39–40: "We cannot begin with complete doubt. . . . Initial skepticism will be a mere self-deception, and not real doubt." See also Peirce, "What Pragmatism Is," in Wiener, *Charles S. Peirce: Selected Writings*, 180, 188–90 (describing radical doubt as "make-believe").

30. Posner, *Problematics of Moral and Legal Theory*, 18.

31. Ibid.

32. Ibid., 12.

33. Ibid., 8.

34. Ibid., 62–63.

35. Percy Bysshe Shelley, "A Defense of Poetry or Remarks Suggested by an Essay Entitled 'The Four Ages of Poetry,'" in *Shelley's Poetry and Prose*, ed. Donald H. Reiman and Sharon B. Powers (New York: W. W. Norton & Co., 1977), 480.

36. Ibid., 488.

37. Ibid., 487. For Dewey's thoughts concerning this passage, see John Dewey, "Art as Experience," in *John Dewey: The Later Works, 1925–1953*, ed. Jo Ann Boydston (Carbondale: Southern Illinois University Press, 1987), 10:329, 347–48, 250.

38. Posner, *Problematics of Moral and Legal Theory*, ix.

39. Ibid., 43.

40. Ibid., ix.

41. Ibid., 42.

42. Ibid., 44.

43. Ibid., 5. ("The members of the family think that the kind of moral theorizing nowadays considered rigorous in university circles has an important role to play in improving the moral judgments and moral behavior of people.")

44. Ibid., 80.

45. Ibid., 6. See also notes 19–23 and accompanying text.

46. Ibid., 32.

47. Ibid.

48. Ibid., xiii.

49. Ibid.

50. Ibid.

51. Ibid.

52. Ibid., 6.

Chapter 4. Rethinking Democracy

1. "Rethinking Democracy" was a response to a paper given by Soares, who was in residence at the University of Virginia during 1995–96—*Eds.*

Chapter 5. First Projects, Then Principles

1. John Rawls, *A Theory of Justice* (Cambridge, MA: Harvard University Press, 1971), 60.

Chapter 6. Does Being an American Give One a Moral Identity?

1. Williams James, "Address on the Philippine Question," in *Essays, Comments, and Reviews (The Works of William James)*, ed. Frederick Burkhardt and Fredson Bowers (Cambridge, MA: Harvard University Press, 1987), 85.

2. Ibid., 86.

3. Edgar Lee Masters, *Spoon River Anthology* (New York: MacMillan, 1915), 102–3.

4. Herbert Croly, *The Promise of American Life* (New York: Capricorn Books, 1964 [1909]), 88.

5. Ibid., 453.

6. Ibid., 2.

7. Ibid., 23.

8. Ibid., 5.

9. Nelson Lichtenstein, *The Most Dangerous Man in Detroit: Walter Reuther and the Fate of American Labor* (New York: Basic Books, 1994), 383.

Chapter 7. Demonizing the Academy

1. Richard Bernstein, *Dictatorship of Virtue: How the Battle over Multiculturalism Is Reshaping Our Schools, Our Country, and Our Lives* (New York: Vintage Books, 1994), 230.

2. See Allan Bloom, *The Closing of the American Mind: How Higher Education Has Failed Democracy and Impoverished the Souls of Today's Students* (New York: Simon and Schuster, 1987)—*Eds.*

Chapter 8. American Universities and the Hope for Social Justice

1. Posner, *Law, Pragmatism, and Democracy*, 155–56.

2. William James, "The Social Value of the College-Bred," in Burkhardt and Bowers, *Essays, Comments, and Reviews*, 109–10.

3. Ibid., 111.
4. Ibid.
5. Ibid., 109.
6. Ibid.

Chapter 10. Can American Egalitarianism
Survive a Globalized Economy?

1. Edward Luttwak, "Why Fascism is the Wave of the Future," *London Review of Books*, April 7, 1994, 3–6—*Eds.*
2. George Orwell, *1984* (New York: Harcourt, Brace and Company, 1949), 166—*Eds.*
3. 1994 Ruffin Lectures in Business Ethics—*Eds.*

Chapter 11. Back to Class Politics

1. John J. Sweeney, with David Kusnet, *America Needs a Raise: Fighting for Economic Security and Social Justice* (Boston: Houghton Mifflin, 1996)—*Eds.*

Chapter 13. Looking Backwards
from the Year 2096

1. From the article "Socialism," by the labor historian Sean Wilentz, in the first edition of *A Companion to American Thought*, ed. Richard Wrightman Fox and James T. Kloppenberg (Malden, MA: Blackwell, 1995), 367–41. That edition appeared exactly one hundred years before the current one, which contains the article "Fraternity," excerpted here. Whereas the first edition contained no essay on fraternity, the latest edition has neither an essay on socialism nor one on rights. (For the full text of "Fraternity," see *A Companion to American Thought*, 7th ed., ed. Cynthia Rodriguez, S.J., and Youzheng Patel [London and New York: Blackwell, 2095], 247–98.)
2. Alexis de Tocqueville, *Democracy in America*, ed. J. P. Mayer, trans. George Lawrence (New York: Harper & Row, 1966), 179—*Eds.*

Chapter 14. The Unpredictable
American Empire

1. Michael Ignatieff, "The Burden," *New York Times*, January 5, 2003, https://www.nytimes.com/2003/01/05/magazine/the-american-empire-the-burden.html.
2. Rorty, *Achieving Our Country*.

3. Gene Wise, "'Paradigm Dramas' in American Studies: A Cultural and Institutional History of the Movement," *American Quarterly* 31, no. 3 (1979): 293–337.

4. David A. Hollinger, *Postethnic America: Beyond Multiculturalism* (New York: Basic Books, 1995).

5. Todd Gitlin, *The Twilight of Common Dreams: Why America Is Wracked by Culture Wars* (New York: Metropolitan Books, 1995); Arthur M. Schlesinger, *The Disuniting of America*, The Larger Agenda Series (Knoxville: Whittle Direct Books, 1991); Rorty, *Achieving Our Country*.

6. Nikhil Pal Singh, "Culture/Wars: Recoding Empire in an Age of Democracy," *American Quarterly* 50, no. 3 (1998): 471–522.

7. David Hollinger, "Foreign Area Studies and the Promise of a More Comprehensive Scholarly Engagement with the United States," *Transit Circle; Revista da Associação Brasileira de Estudos Americanos*, 1999. Hollinger argued that American Studies programs should not think of themselves as developing a distinct scholarly discipline of that name, replete with a method and a central task, but rather on the model of what are called "area studies programs" in the United States—loose assemblages of people from different disciplines who share a common interest in a certain part of the world.

8. Janice A. Radway, "What's in a Name? Presidential Address to the American Studies Association, 20 November 1998," *American Quarterly* 51, no. 1 (1999): 1–32.

Chapter 15. Post-Democracy

1. Chalmers Johnson, *The Sorrows of Empire: Militarism, Secrecy, and the End of the Republic* (New York: Owl Books, 2004), 367.

Chapter 17. Half a Million Blue Helmets?

1. The Belgrade Circle is made up of people who resisted Tito's authoritarianism, and who are now resisting Milosevic's. My visit was sponsored by the Soros Foundation, an organization that Milosevic has now banned from Serbia.

2. Edward Luttwak has redeployed this forgotten German word; it means "gang war," but covers cases in which the gangs consist of hundreds of thousands of men under arms. See his "Great-Powerless Days," *Times Literary Supplement*, June 16, 1995, 9. For the details about what the increasingly selfish American suburbs are doing to the rest of America, see Luttwak's splendid book, *The Endangered American Dream* (New York: Simon & Schuster, 1993).

INDEX

Johnson, Chalmers, 183, 221n1

Johnson, Lyndon, 74, 90–91, 143

justice, 4, 39, 93, 105–6, 115–18, 155, 167, 184, 205, 207, 210. *See also* social justice

Kant, Immanuel, 25, 39, 41–42, 44–45, 47, 51–52, 54, 63, 66, 210

Kerry, John, 35–37, 190

King, Martin Luther, Jr., 12, 37, 59–60, 93, 103, 105, 117, 132, 140, 167

Kozol, Jonathan, 87, 125

Kuhn, Thomas, 56, 58–59, 63

labor, 3–4, 13, 72, 75, 85–86, 89, 95, 104, 113–18, 129–32, 135–37, 138–45, 156, 164–65, 212, 220n1

Left, the, 1, 3, 36–40, 71–77, 110, 112, 115, 119, 123–26, 143–45, 150, 174–76; academic, 3, 8–9, 13–14, 73, 91, 94–96, 97–101, 108, 144–45; cultural, 8–9, 16; radical, 9, 119, 124, 168–69, 173–75, 204–5

Le Pen, Jean-Marie, 141

liberalism, 94, 96, 119–123. *See also* Left, the

Lichtenstein, Nelson, 85, 219n1

Lincoln, Abraham, 83–84, 93, 143, 164, 167, 170

Lind, Michael, 86, 111, 125, 142–43

literature, 6, 43, 62, 100–101, 112, 155–57

Locke, Alan, 5

Luttwak, Edward, 130, 133, 142–43, 220n1, 221n2

MacKinnon, Catharine, 59–61

Margalit, Avishai, 211

Marx, Karl, 33, 60, 129, 167, 209

Masters, Edgar Lee, 83–84, 219n3

McEwan, Ian, 16, 203, 207

Mead, George Herbert, 4

middle class. *See* class, middle

Mill, John Stuart, 54, 61

Misak, Cheryl, 52, 217n11

morality, 33, 53–59, 120–22, 156

moral progress, 6, 47, 50, 53–60, 64, 132, 152–53, 182

multiculturalism, 73, 90–94, 108–9, 111–13, 125, 169, 174

Newton, Isaac, 57–58

Nietzsche, Friedrich, 23–28, 50–51, 61, 209–10, 216n2, 217nn3 and 5–6

Nixon, John, 89, 176

objectivity, 7, 50, 56, 68

Paine, Thomas, 70

Park, Robert, 4

patriotism, 9, 17, 84–86, 89, 94, 165, 170

Peirce, Charles Sanders, 5, 31–32, 55, 218n29

philosophy, 3, 5–7, 11, 21–24, 34–35, 40–45, 50–53, 69–70, 71–72, 128, 209, 211–13; moral, 52, 56–57, 62

Plato, 4, 42, 44–45, 49–51, 64, 122, 210

political correctness, 14, 90, 98–100

politics, 1, 7–9, 21, 65, 77, 112, 151, 204; cultural vs. real, 7–8, 73, 110, 123, 144–45; and philosophy, 3, 6, 10–12, 22, 34, 69, 142. *See also* identity politics

populism, 1, 98–100, 102, 105–7, 117, 130

Posner, Richard, 11–12, 29, 32, 49, 51–63, 98–101, 104, 106, 216n20, 217n15, 218nn25 and 38, 219n1

postmodernism, 12, 65–70, 87, 125, 210–11

pragmatism, 5, 8, 23, 31–32, 49–53, 57–58, 68–70, 215n14

progressivism, 1, 8, 37, 43, 74, 87–88, 104, 122–23

Putnam, Hilary, 62